chess
on the
net

mark crowther

EVERYMAN CHESS

Published by Everyman Publishers plc, London

First published in 2001 by Everyman Publishers plc, Gloucester Mansions, 140A Shaftesbury Avenue, London WC2H 8HD

British Library Cataloguing-in-Publication Data
A catalogue record for this book is available from the British Library.

ISBN 1 85744 237 7

Distributed in North America by The Globe Pequot Press, P.O Box 480, 246 Goose Lane, Guilford, CT 06437-0480

All other sales enquiries should be directed to Everyman Chess, Gloucester Mansions, 140A Shaftesbury Avenue, London WC2H 8HD
tel: 020 7539 7600 fax: 020 7379 4060
email: dan@everyman.uk.com
website: www.everyman.uk.com

EVERYMAN CHESS SERIES (formerly Cadogan Chess)
Chief advisor: Garry Kasparov
Commissioning editor: Byron Jacobs

Typeset and edited by First Rank Publishing, Brighton.
Production by Book Production Services.
Printed and bound in Great Britain by The Cromwell Press Ltd., Trowbridge, Wiltshire.

Contents

Preface

I hope that you find this book useful. The Internet is an unparalleled resource for chess and its future looks bright. I can't imagine any chess player not improving his enjoyment of the game by going on-line. The near future will surely bring more and better chess websites. Faster transmission speeds on the Internet are expected in the relatively near future. This will open up many possibilities for chess with multimedia coverage of events, in its infancy at the moment, being one of them. I expect a huge improvement in the web browsers and chess programs in the next five years. I believe there is a clear niche for an Internet chess program which will allow commentary, chat, quick transmission of moves, text and multimedia. At the moment the expense of producing such a product against the amount of people who might buy it has meant it hasn't happened. I think it can't be too far away though.

If you have any questions about this book then you can email me at **mdcrowth@netcomuk.co.uk**. It is also my intention to have a small website associated with the book. You should look out for it on my pages at **http://www.chesscenter.com/twic/twic.html**.

I must thank all the people who sent me links for the book and the hundreds of people who've given me advice over the years. I hope I've managed to pass at least some good tips on and the encouragement to take a step in cyberspace. I apologise to those whose websites I've inadvertently left out or not given sufficient attention to.

Last of all I must thank John Emms and Byron Jacobs for their tremendous patience. Without their help, encouragement and persuasion this book simply would not have been written.

Mark Crowther
Bradford
April 2001

Chapter One

An Introduction to the Net

What is the Internet?

You can connect computers together to allow the easy transfer of information and files. Sometimes this applies to computers in the same room or the same building. You may have experience of this at work, but the Internet is much wider than that. The Internet connects computers together worldwide and allows them to communicate. More importantly this allows the people who use the computers to communicate. Add into the mix some clever programmers who have produced software to help this process and you end up being able to harness the Internet to do a tremendous number of very interesting things. For example, allowing someone to play chess against another person on the other side of the world.

For a computer to be directly on the Internet there's a complicated procedure requiring connection 24 hours a day and computer expertise beyond the reach of most people. Fortunately there is also another way. The way that most of the millions of people worldwide connect to the Internet is via an Internet Service Provider (ISP), which takes care of the difficult computing tasks required to be part of this global conglomeration of computers. When you sign up with an ISP you are provided with space on their computer. This space is used for collecting any electronic messages you might have been sent (it is a finite space and you can run out if you receive a few huge emails) and storing the files you wish those throughout the world to read. The ISP's computer also provides your live link to the other computers on the internet. When you wish to access the Internet you connect your computer by phone to your ISP's computer and you're ready to go.

History of the Internet

Once connected to your ISP you are connected to a computer that in turn is connected to the Internet. In the 1960's, during the cold war, the US Department of Defence realised that its national computer network was becoming vital. They also found out that if one computer in the network failed it had a knock-on effect to all the others in the system. The cold war made them realise that this was a very unsatisfactory situation and they looked to design a new network where if one computer failed (or more dramatically, was knocked-out), it wouldn't compromise the rest of the system. Computers that needed to communicate with one another would try one route, and if that didn't work out there would be another route to try. Obviously if computers want to talk to each other then they need to communicate in the same way. The Internet relies upon a series of communication developed from that time. The protocol you will hear much about if you spend time on the Internet is TCP/IP (Transmission Control Protocol/Internet Protocol).

The Internet developed quietly in the 1980's, mainly through the university networks. Among the first to develop was Electronic Mail (or email), which allows you to send messages to individuals, and Usenet Newsgroups, which allow you to send messages readable by a wide community. Protocols were also developed: telnet permits direct communication with other computers in real time, and its relation file transfer protocol (ftp) allows the transmission of files between computers. Alongside this growth of computing there were alternatives such as bulletin boards, and eventually there were systems such as CompuServe, who had their own content and message boards. CompuServe was easy to use, although its content was mostly restricted to CompuServe users; the internet, however, had a bit of a learning curve attached to it.

The real growth of the Internet occurred in the early 1990's and it achieved critical mass around 1994 or 1995. Probably the main driving force behind this was the invention of the World Wide Web, which *is* the Internet to many people. Through the use of browsers you can read web pages set up on computers throughout the world, communicate in real time and download files without ever having to understand such terms as telnet and ftp.

The popularity of the Internet has grown exponentially in recent years. At the start you needed to be something of a computer expert to achieve even the simplest tasks, but things have changed. It has now become big business to software companies, service providers and retailers amongst others. They want as many 'ordinary people' to use the Internet as possible. As a result it has never been easier to connect to the Internet and make good use of it.

If you're interested in the history of the Internet or about its technical aspects then you can follow up this subject at the following sites:

http://www.isoc.org/internet-history/
http://coverage.cnet.com/Content/Features/Techno/Networks/ss01.html

Why use the Internet for Chess?

The Internet could have been designed for chess. Along with the computer database it has actually had a pretty revolutionary effect on the game itself. From the late 1980s chess databases became part of a chess professional's life. The data was, however, quite expensive and updates were sent by post. Nowadays almost every major chess tournament and match can be followed live on the Internet, and the larger international open tournaments are updated daily, or at the very latest all the games are presented a few days after end of the event. Chess opening ideas played in the in one time zone might very well be repeated in another part of the world later in the day. As well as this, almost every single significant tournament in chess history is available on the Internet. There are well over two million individual games available on the Internet. Some of the data isn't perfect but much of this data is free and anyone can make use of it. Combined with a chess database, this enables even an average player to be able to appreciate grandmaster games better as they have almost all the material they would ever need.

Once you have the power of a modern computer you can harness the Internet along with a chess playing program and a database to do things you could never dream of doing before. During the recent Brain Games World Chess Championships between Garry Kasparov and Vladimir Kramnik you were be able to see the moves played live. You could feed these into your database and pull out games that have been played before. You were able to see precisely the point where a new move was played, and using a chess program alongside your own chess knowledge, have a pretty good idea of the assessment of the position as the moves came through. The Brain Games website had live pictures from the venue, so you could see the players in action. Along with these pictures there was live audio commentary. If you were a member of an on-line chess server, it was highly likely that they too demonstrated the game. Some of these had a number of grandmasters commentating live on the game. As well as this, on the chess server you would be able to discuss the game with other people just like you. After the game finished, or certainly by the following morning, you were be able to visit other websites where considered annotations by strong grandmasters appeared. In the case of the Brain Games match there was even brief commentary by the team of assistants helping Kasparov and Kramnik (and they often did not agree). Whilst this kind of coverage is most detailed for a world championship match, it is also pretty standard for any elite event taking place throughout the year. Never in history has it been possible to follow the chess circuit in such detail.

If you play chess at a local chess club, with the same opponents, year in year out, and want a change, there is something for you on the Internet too. Whilst it is not possible to recreate the ticking clock and the pleasure of taking someone on over the board, the Internet offers a different set of pleasures. There are hundreds of thousands of players who play chess live on the Internet. You can get a game day or night, twenty-four hours a day if you want. If you're in need of stronger (or perhaps weaker) opposition then the opportunity is there. You can try out new openings or a new style well away from prying eyes. It isn't just playing chess on-line either: just like any other chess club you can chat about anything you'd like to on-line. If you find the right club you'll discover that you can have discussions with people just like you.

In fact the Internet as a whole can be seen as a number of communities. If you go to the right places you'll find people with the same interests as you and with whom you can share knowledge or idle chat.

The World Wide Web has allowed professional and amateur alike to share personal research and interests. Chess programmers for years have met on-line for years to discuss how to get computers to play better chess. Some of the products of their work have been made available on-line for free.

Chess on the Net

If I'm curious about something I see on television or have read in the newspaper I often search the World Wide Web for more information. You can also go to Newsgroups or to bulletin boards and post questions. I've often had the answer to something that has puzzled me for years answered in a few minutes in this way.

You can also read some fantastic articles on chess on-line. In researching this book, I've often been delayed for several hours when I've come across a site I haven't used before and found some absolutely brilliant articles or research.

There are many commercial enterprises on the Internet: it's certainly never been easier to buy chess books and products. When I was a teenager I used to scour second hand bookshops for chess books. Almost certainly you can find such items within minutes on the Internet, seconds if the book is in print.

Commercial software companies want you to buy their products. They often offer great back up and additions to their programs via their own websites.

Above all, remember that although the Internet can be a very passive experience, where you visit websites, read information and download games, you will be missing a lot by not exploring other areas. It's the sending of emails, finding of friends, chatting on-line and the use of chess newsgroups that makes the experience more alive. There are many people who, with a few minutes of their time, can give invaluable advice, pointers as to where to find information or just chat over a recent game of interest. As you find your way around you will see that some sites are more reliable than others are. You will meet some incredibly helpful and knowledgeable people; equally you will meet some less likeable people. That's just part of the medium.

To sum up, if you're interested in chess then the Internet is probably the greatest single set of resources there has ever been, and it's all within a short reach. Here's just a brief summary of what you can do:

- Play chess against players throughout the World, real time.
- Play correspondence chess using email.
- Keep up with the latest chess events, often with live games, involving the World's best players.
- Access hundreds of free chess related programs.
- Access the latest rating lists.
- Buy books and chess equipment.
- Make new friends throughout the World and discuss anything to do with chess.
- Ask advice on anything.
- Contact chess magazines, book publishers, software publishers and even top players.
- Read articles on chess by some of the best chess writers.
- Hear the latest chess news first.
- Publicise your own chess events.
- Learn how to program your own chess-playing computer.
- Get some chess coaching or download opening articles.
- Find out about chess tournaments, contact the organisers and perhaps enter.
- Read reviews on chess books and software.

- Access millions of chess games for use in chess database programs.
- Get support for your favourite programs with updates and free services.
- Contact national or international chess federations.

How to Get up and Running

If you're inspired to use the Internet, what do you need?

First of all you require a computer. There are, however, many types of computer. When I first learned of the Internet I was working at a University. I used their computer system that utilised an operating system called UNIX. This was the dominant type of computer accessing the Internet until the early 1990's. Nowadays the IBM Personal Computer (PC) is the dominant computer system and if you're starting from scratch you should strongly consider buying one of these. There are also Apple Macs and many people swear by them, as they are in many ways easier to use. But be aware that many chess programs you might want to use from the Internet won't work on Apple Macs. It's a sad fact of life.

When buying a computer, try and go for at the very least a computer in the mid-price range. The pat advice is to go for the most expensive one you can afford. You can still access the Internet using really quite old computers, but it can become a very frustrating exercise after a while. I have always bought from a local company that builds its own computers. I found I got plenty of help and support when I got stuck in the early years. This is fine, of course, if you can find a company that you trust, but be warned: there are also plenty of cowboys.

Whenever you buy a computer find out what kind of technical support you can expect. Mostly you'll choose either a high street or mail order computer. These mass-market computers are fine, especially if you take some time to research them. There are numerous monthly magazines that review computers, the latest updates and the best buys at low, medium and high prices. They will give you very sound advice and help you to avoid buying a real stinker. If you know people with a bit of expertise that can help you choose your computer, then so much the better.

Modems

Along with the computer you will also need a modem. This is a device that allows you to connect to another computer using a standard phone line. Modems are determined by the speed at which they send and receive information. You should go for a 56.6KBs (56,000 bytes per second), which is the fastest modem that will probably ever work reliably with normal phone lines. However, already new sorts of data and phone lines that work far quicker are being installed, especially if you live in the United States. You should check with your phone company (or cable company) to see if you have a new digital high-speed-data-line instead of an analogue phone line, because if you have you'll need to get a different modem to get the best out of it. The faster the speed of connection you have to the Internet, the better, believe me.

Internet Service Providers

The next item on your list is an Internet Service Provider. These days you'll probably get a disk to a recommended ISP with your computer. There are also start-up disks on the front of many computing magazines, and some of them are even free. Understand you do get what you pay for. A free ISP is a relatively new phenomenon and may not be around forever. They rely on getting a large number of subscribers, and with that they hope to sell advertising and other products to their customers. It's hard to tell whether this is a sound commercial proposition in the long term, but it does at least grant someone who is new to the idea of the Internet the chance to experiment at no cost. Again there are computing or internet magazines that specialise in telling you the best offers and reviewing the services provided. As a one off purchase they're quite cheap and worth consulting. One thing to remember is the cost of phone calls: you need to make sure you're making your calls at either no cost or the lowest possible cost (local rate calls). For that your ISP will either have to be a local company, have a local POP (Point of presence) or a special rate phone line.

Computing Knowledge

I won't lie and say that no computing knowledge is required to use the Internet, but it's certainly possible to become proficient relatively quickly. I've learned a lot over the years bit by bit, but I found getting started reasonably easy, and that was at a time when it was pretty hard to use the Internet. You do need to have a basic concept of what is going on, what files are and how to use windows programs in general. From this to run something like an internet browser is an easy step. If you are at a very basic stage, then you should either ask someone to show you the first steps or buy a simple beginner's book. However, in the end the only way to learn is to just jump in and practice.

Chapter Two

Essential Knowledge

In this chapter we will be taking a brief look at the more technical side of 'Chess on the Net'. While it's true that you can use the Internet without any real understanding of it, it also must be said that you're far more likely to enjoy all its benefits with a little knowledge behind you.

Software Required

Most of the basic software you need to start out on-line comes as standard with your computer. If you have Microsoft Windows you will have a suite of programs that work together. Microsoft Internet Explorer is their web browser. This works in conjunction with Outlook Express, their email and newsgroup program. Once you have basic access to the Internet you can go about getting other programs which may suit your purposes better.

There are sites that specialise in giving basic advice and reviews on software you might need. The best of these are **www.about.com** and **cnet.com**.

E-mail

E-mail (or email) is an abbreviation of electronic mail, a system of sending messages by electronic means from one computer user to one or more recipients via a network.

As far as required software goes, Microsoft Windows includes the aforementioned Outlook Express, while other emailing software includes Pegasus Mail, Eudora and USENET readers.

As webmaster of TWIC, the first thing I do every day is to read my overnight emails. There are a number of different categories of email you can receive.

1) Emails written directly to you.

2) Discussion groups that you sign up for, such as the chess list.

3) Distribution lists that you sign up for. This contains information you request from companies. They might tell you of special offers or updates to a website. I regularly receive chess related emails from chess.about.com, kasparovchess.com and chesscafe.com.

4) Material you receive because you are on a list from a chess organiser or event. If you do distribute information or articles to a large number of people, you should learn how to send these emails as a blind copy. A blind copy is where an email is sent to a large number of individuals, but only the individual's address appears in the header of the email he or she receives. I regularly receive emails with the addresses of around a hundred or more other people in the header. This makes the email much larger than it has to be. Not to mention it might give addresses of your friends away, when they'd rather they were kept private.

5) An email from a complete stranger or organisation you've never heard of. There are many ways to get hold of an email address. It can be collected from your own web page, contributions to a discussion in the newsgroups or bought from a company that you have done business with on the Internet. These emails are mainly of no interest whatsoever and you should be especially careful of any attachments they have.

Attachments – A Warning!

Emails are plain text. That is, the raw message you receive will consist of only letters, some limited symbols and numbers, and will have a width of not more that 64 characters. In this plain form emails cannot carry viruses or do damage to your computer. Anyone who tells you differently is wrong.

However, it was realised long ago that people would like to send programs, word-processing files and innumerable other types of computer file in what is known as the binary format. As emails only transmit plain text, a method had to be found to convert these binary files into plain text format. Your email client normally reads these MIME attachments automatically and displays them below the message.

Once you decide to open these attachments they are turned into binary files. It's then possible that these files, if they are malevolent programs or viruses, can cause damage to your computer. You have to decide as to whether to open these files on an individual basis. In general, if they are from a complete stranger and don't relate to you in any way, you should not open them. Even if they are apparently from friends, but the email is not a personal one, they can be viruses. It's possible their system has been infected with a virus, which then replicates itself by using their address book to send the virus onto their friends. You should, in any case, have an anti-virus program installed on your computer. These programs detect the most common problem files and viruses and stop them doing the damage they were intended to do.

Advice about Sending Attachments

As a chess journalist I receive many files a week via email, containing pictures, news, chess data files and programs, amongst other things. Many take a long time to download (because they can be very large) and are awkward to deal with (because they contain many files). Many of these problems can be avoided with a little thought from the sender.

Picture files and word processing files can be made much smaller by using the zip utility. Zip programs (an example is winzip at **http://www.winzip.com**) are compression programs. That is, it takes files and reduces them in size. You should never send huge files un-zipped if they can be substantially reduced in size by zipping them. Word processing files such as Microsoft Word files can be reduced by huge amounts by compression. However, you should also consider whether such files should be sent at all. Word processing files retain certain information such as paragraph formats, tables, fonts and so forth. If the file only contains textual information you should consider sending it as plain text (copy and paste into a text file or save as a text file within the program).

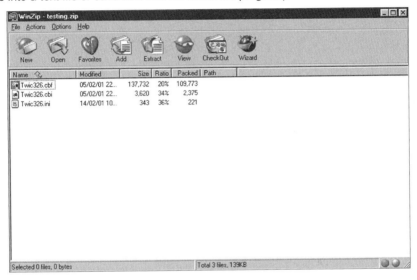

The always useful Winzip utility

Zipping files has another purpose too. If you send a large number of files, it is much eas-ier for the receiver to unzip one file than individually open a large number of attachments.

There are two categories of chess file that should be compressed. PGN files of games are a plain text format. There is some merit in leaving them unzipped if they only contain a few games, as it's easier for someone to see what they are directly from their email client. If they are large files it is only polite to zip them, as their size can be reduced by around 70%, which makes it quicker both for you to send them and for your intended recipient to download them.

There are two formats of ChessBase file. The old ChessBase format has only two vital files (.cbf and .cbi; even then I have a utility to create the .cbi file if missing) and the new ChessBase 6 format (.cbh is the name of the main file but this will not work on its own – if you send this file to another person you need to send the other related files). The Chess-Base 6 format has many files, almost all of which are vital if the data is to be read by the person you are sending it to. You have two choices in order to send these files in a friendly way. Firstly you could zip them all together and send them. This is fine. However there is a second very efficient way. ChessBase has its own compression program built in. By using its 'Archive Database' option, a single file (.cbv) can be created which can be sent over the Internet. The receiver is able to use ChessBase to restore the archive.

In general, if you want to send an announcement to a large number of people, then try and keep the size of the announcement small. A brief message, with the key points you want to make in conjunction with a reference to a website with fuller details, is by far the most effective method. Remember that many people refuse to open files such as Microsoft Word documents that are sent to them by complete strangers.

Practice Safe Downloading

One of the first things you should do is to purchase a virus scan program. It makes sense to have protection against nasty surprises in your email and also over the Internet. It is especially true if you are intending to do a lot of downloading of programs and zipped files. Having said that, viruses are pretty rare from respectable chess sites. If you want to go to underground sites for hacked versions of programs you're in the wild country of the Internet. I personally prefer to stick to commercial products, although I have tested freeware programs with no problems. There is the possibility both from commercial and non-commercial programs (and the more you load the more the danger) of causing your computer problems due to conflicts between programs. If you have bought a commercial program and it causes such a problem you have every right to complain.

Making Use of the World Wide Web

There are a huge number of chess related websites. I imagine that I'm not alone in having a number of core sites that I consult regularly for business and pleasure, and then, depending on current events or interest, I widen the number of sites I take in.

The first thing you need is a web browser. There are two major alternatives: Internet Explorer (IE), which will already be installed on your computer if you use Microsoft Windows, and Netscape. There are alternatives programs such as Opera and NeoPlanet, as well as iCab for the Mac, all of which are more than acceptable. There is also a very old DOS based browser called Lynx which is useful for sites which are extremely slow, although using this program is not for the inexperienced.

Microsoft Internet Explorer dominates the market. After all, if you have a browser on your computer why would you change? At the time of writing 86% of web surfers use the Internet Explorer. This means that for one thing, every page designer checks his or her pages on IE but not necessarily Netscape. Nevertheless, Netscape is also a fine product and worth checking out to see if you prefer it. IE and Netscape aren't merely Web browsers; they also include software for reading and sending email and USENET messages. They're always trying to outdo each other. It's a good reason to want to see some competition in this area.

It's worth pointing out why there's a battle to give away free software. Many people don't know how to customise their web browsers for their own needs. Each browser, especially in its unaltered state, will recommend sites that are either especially designed for the browser or have commercial agreements with the manufacturer. This adds up to incredible advertising potential. By learning even a little about browsers you can customise it to meet your needs. You should definitely start by changing the default home page. Change it to a site that you want to see loaded up, not the default Netscape, Microsoft or in certain cases, your ISP's homepage. In the case of ISPs, sometimes you receive a disk from a service provider that includes the latest browser software and a whole package of material to enable you to use their service. This may include sending you by default to places where they have commercial relationships.

You can read reviews of internet browsers on sites such as cnet.com. This site will keep you up to date with the development of the different versions of the browsers and any problems that have been encountered. Whilst you can download the latest versions of internet browsers on-line, it does take some time. The latest versions of browser programs are often made available to the public via CD ROMs attached to computing magazines. It's often worth considering using this relatively cheap route to upgrade to the latest editions of the programs you use the most. Also there are some very good internet magazines about; it's a good place to start improving your knowledge.

Review

Site Name: CNET.com
URL: http://www.cnet.com and http://www.help.com

This American based site (subtitled 'The source for computers and technology') is one of the longest established sites on the Internet. It is a wonderful resource, with advice on how to use the Internet and on computing in general. It also provides a huge set of links to commercial, shareware and freeware programs that are available.

You should definitely consult the Software Reviews section on the Internet for the latest news on browsers, email clients and general internet utilities. Another important part of the site is their help section. Although it is part of the same site it has a different internet address: **http://www.help.com**.

The chess software section is limited to freeware and shareware programs. There are far better guides available elsewhere on the Internet. My only problem with this site is that it can sometimes be difficult to find your way around. Part of the confusion is due to the site's structure, with the Software Reviews, Help & How To and Free Downloads section covering some of the same ground. However, there is a search facility that certainly helps with some of these problems. If you find the advice given on this site too complex then you should try about.com.

Review

Site Name: About.com
URL: http://www.about.com

This site doesn't just offer advice about computers, software and the Internet. It offers advice about almost any subject you can think of. The guides are written by a series of subject editors. You can ask them questions; there are forums to discuss the subjects too. **http://netforbeginners.about.com** is their basic guide to the Internet, with articles such as: 'Do you need more than one browser, and by the way, what's a browser?'

There are two problems I have with this site. Firstly, it has built up over the years; some advice was good when it was given, but can be a bit out of date by the time you come to read it. Secondly, the way they link to other sites is simply horrible. Instead of directly linking to recommended sites they use their about.com to surround the target site. This means that sometimes it isn't easy to find out where you've been sent, and it also can make it hard to get the best out of the site you're visiting.

Their chess section is available at **http://chess.about.com**, which is excellent and will be discussed elsewhere.

About.com Guides Questions Specific To:	**Ab⊕ut**⊚
AOL	Ask Our About.com Guide to AOL, Sharon Gillson -- Click Here.
Chatting	Ask Our About.com Guide to Chatting, Julie Martin -- Click Here.
Clip Art	Ask Our About.com Guide to Web Clip Art, Bobbie Peachey -- Click Here.
Computer Reviews	Ask Our About.com Guide to Computer Reviews, J. Newberry -- Click Here.
Email	Ask Our About.com Guide to Email, Heinz Tschabitscher -- Click Here.

about.com – advice on just about any subject you can think of

Understanding How Internet Pages and Links Work

It's important to have a basic understanding on how web pages and links work.

A web address is sometimes also known as a URL (Universal Resource Locator). The URL can be split into several parts. To show this I'm going to take the example of about.com, whose URL is **http://www.about.com**.

This consists of the following parts:

http:// – This stands for HyperText Transfer Protocol. Most web addresses have this at the front, but not all. Web addresses can start differently as this merely describes the method to be used to access the document. Some web addresses can start ftp:// and that stands for File Transfer Protocol.

www – The files on the Internet are stored on a computer. This computer hosts an internet site. The next part of an internet address signifies that. In the case of about.com the address of the homepage is **http://www.about.com**. Strictly speaking the www is not required in this case, although it is entirely dependent on the way the site has been set up. WWW merely stands for World Wide Web. In the case of about.com they often use other words in its place to direct people to other parts of their site, for example **http://chess.about.com** for the chess part of their site.

about.com – This part of the address is the domain name of about.com. This has been registered with an organisation called InterNIC. InterNIC specially deals with the global domain names .com, .org and .net. Traditionally .com was for commercial sites, .net for organisations involved in internet infrastructure activities, and .org was for non-profit organisations. However many companies register all three to avoid losing traffic to competitors. InterNIC is part of the US Department of Commerce and they administer the process whereby Domain Name Servers can direct requests for a site to the correct computer.

Domain names are not truly owned. Instead they're leased out on a first come first serve basis. They remain with the initial applicant unless they are not renewed, or another company can demonstrate a greater right to the address than the original leaseholder. The leases can also be sold on to a third party. Domain names can be registered up to 10 years in advance in blocks of one year. They are registered with official registrars who have to be members of an organisation called ICANN (Internet Corporation for Assigned Names and Numbers).

You might want to read more about this at Internic's website at **http://rs.internic.net** and at ICANN's website at **http://www.icann.org**. In addition to the global .net, .com and .org sites, there are others administered by individual countries. For example, we have .uk for the United Kingdom, .de for Germany and .ru for Russia. They have different rules and are administered by a different body. They are supposed to be kept for residents of these individual countries.

Once a company has a domain name it can then go ahead and put its material on-line. Each computer on the Internet has its own address. It is called an IP address and it is just a string of numbers. For instance About.com's IP address is 209.143.212.20. If you place this number in a browser window you will see that it brings up the About.com homepage.

There is a DOS program called ping that may very well be automatically on your computer. One method of discovering an IP address is to type (in the case of about.com):

ping about.com

and it will give you the address and some statistics about how fast the site is operating.

Frequently a company will not host its own website but get a specialist company to do it for them. When you register a domain name you are also given the opportunity to change the IP address. So you can place your website on one hosting computer and inform the licensing authorities. Later, if you change hosting companies, you can inform the licensing authorities and they will direct traffic for a domain name from one IP address to a new one. When you go to an internet site you enter the domain name and a computer called a DNS (Domain Name Server) will automatically route the request to the correct computer. Sometimes several domain names go to the same IP address. An example of this is that **http://www.kasparovchess.com** and **http://www.kasparov.com** both go to the same site.

My own site *The Week in Chess* (TWIC) is a part of the London Chess Centre site. The address of the London Chess Centre is **http://www.chesscenter.com** and the address of TWIC's site is **http://www.chesscenter.com/twic/twic.html**. This reveals another part of a web address. The /twic is a directory and /twic.html is an HTML (hypertext mark up language) document.

Sometimes the full address of a document doesn't appear on the address bar at the top of the screen. This is usually because a site uses frames. Nevertheless, almost every file and page will have a unique address, but it will be hidden from you because of the way frames work. If you wish to open the document outside frames or link to it, right click on the link to the document. Often if you want to use that address directly, you can right click with the mouse on a link to another page or document and use the option 'Copy Shortcut'. This address can be pasted into the address bar at the top of the page.

Why would this be useful? I've found over the years that this is one of the best ways of getting material from the Internet. For instance, in my coverage of the FIDE 2000 World Chess Championships I had a round 1 file called **http://www.chesscenter.com/twic/event/fide2000/fidech1.pgn**. You could enter this into the address bar at the top of the page and then, after downloading round 1's games, you could change the last part of the address to /fidech2.pgn and reasonably expect it to give the round 2 games. This approach can be useful on sites where there are very long links to a series of files with very similar names, when going back and forth can be very slow.

This approach of editing addresses in the address bar can go a stage further. Sometimes websites allow chess games to be viewed on-line but with no text version of the moves. This means you either have to type in the game move by move yourself or you have to find another way. Often there are PGN files powering these pages; all you have to do is to find out their names. Often the 'hidden' internet address is within the source of the page. The pages are written in the language HTML, which in many cases isn't especially complicated. The browser looks at the source and understands how to display the page. You can 'View-Source' as an option in an internet browser. If you're convinced that a Java viewer is powered by a PGN file you can often find the address of the file within the source. This trick has allowed me to cover many events that would have otherwise been terribly difficult to do.

Internet Search Engines

What do you do if you want to find a specific piece of information on the Internet but don't know where to look?

You use an Internet search engine. The use of search engines is a highly competitive area, as this kind of site is one of the most popular on the Internet and therefore the most lucrative (some of them even make money).

According to a survey by Cyveillance in July 2000 (they have a web-ticker at **http://www.cyveillance.com** which had reached 3.2 billion by the time I reached their site!), there's around 7 million web pages being added each day and over 2.2 billion pages altogether. With this in mind, everyone can use some help to find material. Search engines work on a number of different principles and your choice should depend on the task you want to achieve.

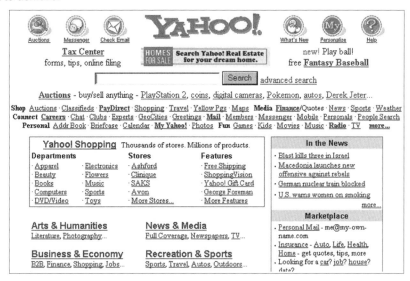

www.yahoo.com – a major search engine on the web

There are three major approaches used by search engines, depending upon how the index (or indexes) they use is compiled.

A Web Directory is a list of sites arranged by category where information can be found. These are often compiled by hand and some directories have reviews. When you search a site such as this, the first sites you are shown are ones in the directory. Another approach is to solicit people to submit information about their websites to the directory. A whole industry has grown up around the submission of such information. Companies say that with their help they will get your website highly rated in these directories. Examples of Web Directories are:

http://www.yahoo.com
http://www.looksmart.com
http://www.snap.com

The second category indexes individual pages on the Internet. They will either index the full text of individual pages or make use of hidden text at the top of a page called a Meta Tag. Some, but not all search engines index Meta Tags, and it is a method by which the webmaster can control the way that his site is represented. However, they are widely abused in attempts to get pages listed when they might otherwise not be, and because of this many website databases are starting to ignore or place less trust upon them in the ranking of pages. Examples of straightforward search engines are:

http://www.google.com
http://www.altavista.com
http://www.northernlight.com
http://www.lycos.com

A third category is the Meta Engine. These sites submit search queries to a number of the major search engines and then process and present the results. They do have a number of disadvantages in that they don't usually have an agreement to use all the major databases, don't submit your query to the target engines quite as you formulated it and tend only to use the first 30 or so results from each engine. However, they are great for looking for single rare words or names. Examples of Meta Engines are:

http://www.dogpile.com
http://infind.com
http://www.metacrawler.com

At the time of researching this book the most popular search engines were, according to the Nielsen/Net Ratings, as follows:

Yahoo	**http://www.yahoo.com**	47%
MSN	**http://www.msn.com**	35.8%
Go (Infoseek)	**http://www.go.com**	19.1%
Netscape	**http://www.netscape.com**	15.4%
Lycos	**http://www.lycos.co.uk**	14.4%
AltaVista	**http://www.altavista.com**	12.3%
Excite	**http://www.excite.com**	11.7%
LookSmart	**http://www.looksmart.com**	8.1%
Snap	**http://www.nbci.com**	7.6%
GoTo	**http://www.goto.com**	6.8%
iWon	**http://www.iwon.com**	6.7%
Google	**http://www.google.com**	3.8%
HotBot	**http://www.hotbot.lycos.co.uk**	3.7%
AskJeeves	**http://www.ask.com**	3.4%
DirectHit	**http://www.directhit.com**	2.1%
WebCrawler	**http://www.webcrawler.com**	1.8%
Northern Light	**http://www.northernlight.com**	1.3%
Open Directory	**http://www.dmoz.org**	0.8%
Raging Search (from Alta Vista)	**http://ragingsearch.altavista.com**	0.1%

Note: Because a web surfer may visit more than one service, the combined totals exceed 100 percent.

These figures can be a bit misleading, certainly in actually rating the effectiveness of a search engine. Sites such as MSN and Netscape are the default search engines for the Microsoft Internet Explorer and the Netscape browsers respectively. Users who don't change their start pages will use them almost by default.

An additional factor is that some of the companies are related (for instance Alta Vista and Raging Search), offering similar services aimed at different audiences.

Indexing the Internet is an expensive business, especially if the results are to be up-to-date. If the index is slow to be compiled and rechecked then firstly, they will not turn up recent documents and secondly, they will send you to pages that no longer exist (so called 'dead links').

If you're looking for something, how do you start?

As this is primarily a chess book, I will use examples from the chess world.

Firstly, you ought to consider if you really need to use a search engine at all. If you are looking for a major personality or company it may be enough to just guess the address. For instance, if you were searching for Garry Kasparov's internet site then you could just type in the toolbar at the top

http://www

follow it with Kasparov's name to get

http://www.kasparov

and then add .com to get

http://www.kasparov.com.

This would actually lead you to his commercial internet site.

This does, however, bring an interesting point to the fore. Kasparov's chess site is in fact called kasparovchess.com. Many years ago someone registered Kasparov's name and started a site at the address **kasparov.com**. Kasparov had to go through the courts to win back the rights to his name! A year ago the method shown above would not have reached Kasparov's site. Now, however, both the addresses **http://www.kasparov.com** and **http://www.kasparovchess.com** take you to the same place. So whilst this guessing method is a good start, it doesn't always work.

Secondly, you can look in web guides or directories. I will cover in some detail chess links pages elsewhere. The main directory on the Internet is Yahoo (http://www.yahoo.com). I have never particularly liked the chess selection on this site, but it can certainly be used to search for specific sites whose name is already known.

A better guide for chess is offered by **http://www.looksmart.com**. A chess listing which does seems to have the major chess sites can be found by following these directory sections:

Lifestyle > **Hobbies** > **Games & Puzzles** > **Board Games** > **Chess**

Chess on the Net

Elsewhere, I look at **http://chess.about.com**, which is also an interesting place to start, with a mixture of articles and links to other places. One major criticism I have is its infuriating house style of keeping its own banner and address at the top of the browser, making it difficult to know where you have been directed.

How Do You Search the Internet?

If you're looking for an exact piece of information then you'll have to choose one of the major search engines. The links above contain nearly all the major ones available. Although it's a matter of taste, having researched this section I would recommend Google (**http://www.google.com**) and Raging Search (**http://ragingsearch.altavista.com**). The latter is a new way of accessing AltaVista, which you can customise to your own taste.

For many years I got by just putting a couple of words into a search engine and seeing what came out. This approach still works, provided you use a little intelligence in choosing the right words. Even searching for 'Chess' will get you a lot of hits but very much a rag-bag of sites (Google claims to return 1,340,000 hits). Nevertheless you could still use this approach, especially on Google, as it allows you to click on a section called related pages, and in my case it produced a fine list of chess sites. So if you see something that you think is a close match to the kind of site you want to find, you can click on related pages and get a completely new list which is perhaps closer to your intended search.

However, for best results you should search for specific subjects using, if you can, keywords (or even better, combinations of keywords) that are specific to the subject you are looking for. You should also understand that search engines have different policies to common words. Some do not index the most common words such as 'and', 'the' and 'but'; others will only search such stop words if you specifically tell them to.

Most search engines use the following method to allow you to narrow down searches.

If you type in:

Bobby Fischer

depending on the search engine you are using, some will serve you with documents in which Bobby or Fischer are present, but most will only give you documents with both. If you are unsure you can use the formulation:

+Bobby +Fischer

which would definitely give only documents with both words in them.

You also have the option of putting the words in inverted commas. For example:

'Bobby Fischer'

would only serve documents that see the two words appear together.

If you found a lot of documents mentioning Boris Spassky and you didn't want a mention of him you could use the formulation:

+Bobby +Fischer -Spassky

This is good enough for most searches on the Internet.

There is another method of narrowing searches: that is Boolean Algebra. Not all search engines support Boolean logic but it can be very powerful. The commands are AND, OR and NOT (all capitalised). You can also nest the commands using brackets. For instance, if you wanted material on Karpov's matches against Kasparov and Korchnoi you could try:

Karpov AND (Kasparov OR Korchnoi)

AltaVista provides another command NEAR. For example:

Karpov NEAR Kasparov 10

would provide documents where the word Karpov appears within ten words of Kasparov.

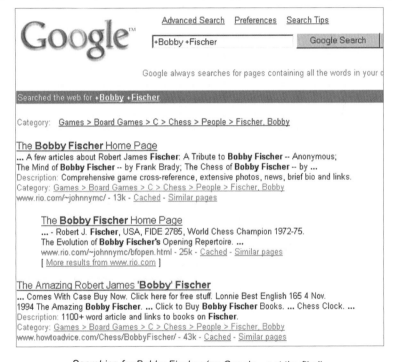

Searching for Bobby Fischer (on Google – not the film!)

It would be incredibly useful to search by date of document. Unfortunately, however, most computers, when asked to provide a date for the document, will either provide a completely random date or the date that the document was indexed.

If you're searching for up-to-date documents it's also worth remembering that the indexing of individual sites is at the very least a month old, and possible much older. Often you will have to use, if available, a search engine for the individual site for the most accurate search of that site. Some sites generate documents only as the result of a query. In that case these documents will not be indexed. Also, any documents in formats such as Microsoft Word or PDF, which require special readers, won't be indexed either. It's simply a case of clever searching and working around these limitations, using a combination of sites that you know contain the kind of information you want.

Read more about Internet Search Engines, reviews and how to use them on the following sites:

http://websearch.about.com/internet/websearch
http://www.searchengineshowdown.com
http://searchenginewatch.internet.com
http://home.cnet.com/internet

Sometimes a topic isn't covered well by a website but has been discussed in the news-groups. If you wish to search USENET postings then the site with the best database is Deja.com **http://www.deja.com/usenet**

Newsgroups

If you want to use the newsgroups then you're going to need a piece of software called a newsgroup reader to do so. They will allow you to connect to the server for Usenet, find the groups you are most interested in and arrange the messages into some sort of order.

The most commonly used newsgroup readers are those that come with the Internet browsers Microsoft Explorer and Netscape Navigator (or Communicator). There is nothing wrong with these and there is plenty of literature to help you to get the best out of them.

There are alternatives: I have a preference for Forte Free Agent, which facilitates reading messages off-line. For that and its fully featured shareware (i.e. you have to pay for it) brother Forte Agent, you can go to the website **http://www.forteinc.com**. Another alterna-tive is the shareware program Microplanet gravity at **http://www.microplanet.com**. These programs have to compete with the Microsoft and Netscape products, so the companies involved are motivated to give their programs useful features. By the time you read this there may be other great programs too. If you decide newsgroups are something you will use regularly then guides such as those available at About.com (**http://usenet.about.com/internet/usenet/mbody.htm**) will keep you up-to-date on develop-ments.

The Usenet Newsgroups are amongst the oldest parts of the Internet. When I started to use the Internet in 1993, they were the primary place to get news and information. They can be insidiously addictive. You can post a question or an opinion that you feel strongly about, and within a few minutes you have started a discussion that goes on for days or weeks. It is interesting to understand a little of how they work. The newsgroups don't exist in one place. Your message should appear almost immediately on the news feed you use; then it is gradually distributed to all the other news servers in the world.

Chess Programs and Chess Files

We already know that to get the best out of the Internet you require a basic knowledge of computing, an understanding of files and of windows programs in general. From this to run something like an internet browser is an easy step.

Then there are more detailed things you need to know. One thing is for sure: A chess program that allows you to play through games is pretty much a prerequisite. There are a number of standard formats for games transmitted on the Internet. PGN (Portable Game Notation) is the internet standard and the main default. However, ChessBase is so dominant that you may see ChessBase files transmitted directly.

If you have a chess-playing program for your PC, you will already have some of the skills required. A database program would be even better. 10 years ago a database program was an expensive item, and acquiring data for it was even more expensive. Nowadays it's different. Chess data, because of its easy availability on the Internet, is very cheap. There are databases of 2 million chess games available for very small prices; the data isn't perfect but it's good enough for most purposes.

Given that computer experts were amongst the first to populate the Internet (after all, you need a computer to access it), they were also the first to start exploiting its potential. In the chess arena programmers developed on-line chess play and a common standard for transmitting chess games (PGN). Many of the World's greatest experts on programming chess computers, people such as Hans Berliner and Feng-hsiung Hsu (founding programmer of Deep Blue), wrote openly in newsgroups and were readily contactable. Projects such as GNU Chess were started, where code for a chess playing program was made available on the Internet. Many people contributed to its improvement, and even more could examine it and get an idea of how to go about the task of programming a computer to play chess.

I know that when I first started on the Internet, I valued most the communication part of the deal. I loved posting news and games to the newsgroups, emailing and chatting on-line to famous and not-so-famous chess players. I didn't enjoy playing against computers and didn't see the need for a database. However, the more you use the Internet, the more you realise that you'd get a whole lot more out of it, firstly with a database program and secondly with a chess playing program. For those who buy chess programs from shops but don't use the Internet, there is even more to gain, with product support available for almost every commercial program.

If you follow chess tournaments for any period of time on the Internet, you'll want a database. There are millions of chess games available for download on the Internet and every week anywhere between 1000 and 5000 games are made available. When examining a game, a combination of a chess database (to look up previous games in the opening variation) and a chess engine (to analyse the position, especially useful in tactical positions) can turn you into an instant chess expert.

Whilst this is a book on internet chess, here I will have to express some opinion on chess programs. Currently I use ChessBase 7 (the latest version ChessBase 8 has just been released) and I have also used ChessAssistant in the past. Both are good programs with all the required features.

Review

Site Name: Chess Program Reviews
URL: http://www.chessreviews.com
Alternative URL: http://www.chessopolis.com/csr/index.htm)
Country: US
Language: English

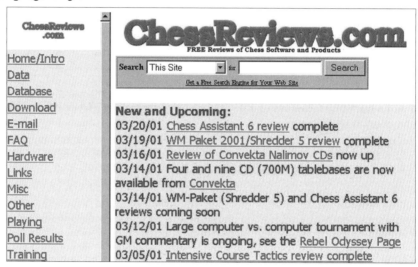

Authors Description

This site provides reviews of all the major and commercial chess software packages. Other things you can find on the site include informative articles on computer chess related subjects, software polls and book information.

My comments

Bob Pawlak's site is a fine example of a fan site that has turned into something more. He freely admits to being only of moderate strength as an over-the-board player, but has gained a reputation as a person who writes interesting and well thought out reviews of (mostly commercial) software.

His site is structured reasonably clearly, with the left bar linking to sections covering, amongst others, chess database, playing and training programs. When you click on these left sidebar links you get another set of links to the reviews themselves. In the centre on the homepage is simply a list of the latest changes made to the site, new reviews and stories about upcoming products.

Of course, reviewing commercial software is a very subjective matter; nevertheless when deciding on what to purchase it's useful to get all the advice you can get. As he has been reviewing software for a number of years now the site is starting to become quite comprehensive. You can track the development of a program through his reviews of the different versions. It might be that you have the opportunity to buy an older version of a program and want to know what it is like. There is certainly no law against buying older products and indeed it's a very good way to save money, especially if you're not that fussy about having the best, but merely something functional. Also, it allows you to refer back to the old reviews and compare old with new, without rehashing elements of the program that remain unchanged. The comparisons also allow you to decide whether to upgrade from one program to another.

The reviews themselves are the outstanding part of the site. Starting from a general standpoint, he describes what the program does first, whether it has any significant bugs and gives a tentative view. He follows this by going into some detail listing the capabilities, particularly when there is more than one product in the area and the differences might be important. Then he outlines the strengths and weaknesses as he sees them overall. He finally outlines whether there is any copy protection on the program.

If you want to purchase a piece of chess software then this is a good place to start on your search.

Review

Site Name: About.com on Chess Databases
URL: http://chess.about.com/games/chess/cs/databases/index.htm
Country: US
Language: English

My Comments

This contains some of the basics about chess databases. However, this area of the site wasn't as up to date as I might have liked.

Portable Game Notation (PGN) and other Chess Files

PGN is a standard that was organised and promoted by Stephen J Edwards in the early 1990s. At the simplest level, you can save PGN files from all over the Internet and play through the games on almost any chess software. PGN files replaced the old format ChessBase files as the standard on the Internet.

PGN files are text. You can read them in any text editor or word processor. The fact they are text and not binary files means that they cannot carry viruses and can be read by any operating system (PC, Mac or UNIX).

There are other format files you will see on the Internet. ChessBase files are the most common: cbf·and cbi files are old ChessBase format, while cbh and the index files are the modern ChessBase format. The new option is a compressed ChessBase format (cbv) and this should be used when sending games in new ChessBase format. You may also occasionally come across ChessAssistant, TascBase and NicBase files.

Most chess software now read PGN files directly, while almost all offer to convert them into their own format.

There is some merit in learning how to edit PGN files manually in a text editor. You can mass replace headers, dates, insert round numbers and generally tidy up PGN files this way. You can also place the games in whatever order you want by cutting and pasting (more about this in Chapter 4).

Free Database Programs

Following are details of the best known free database programs.

Review

Scid (Shane's Chess Information Database)

This is a free chess database application for Unix and Microsoft Windows operating systems, written by Shane Hudson. I found it quite easy to download and set up on a Windows 98 computer. It's available at **http://members.xoom.com/sghudson**. You also need to have an additional package called Tcl/Tk, available at **http://dev.scriptics.com/software/tcltk/download83.html**. Note that new versions of the Tcl/Tk software may be produced, but I'm sure the Scid site will make the necessary alterations to the link it gives.

Review

ChessBase Light.

There are very few demo versions of commercial programs that don't drive you up the wall after a short period of time. Of course, that is their purpose! A demo gives you a feel for a commercial program, but the limitations should encourage you to part with your money for the product.

ChessBase Light is a little better than that. It's a special version of ChessBase 6.0, which can be freely downloaded. It's limited to 8000 games per database and supports both the PGN format and the new CBH format of ChessBase 6 and Fritz5. Within the 8000 games barrier there is no limit to save, copy, convert, annotate, print, search, analyse, merge and classify games. It's a pretty good starting point if you have no budget. This can be obtained at **http://www.chessbase.com/Products/cblight/index.htm**.

Review

CDB1.5

This is a database program written by Peter Klausler. This is reviewed at **http://www.chessopolis.com/csr/cdb_10.htm** and the download is on the same site at http://www.chessopolis.com/cdb-1_5.exe. It is quite old but has all the essential attributes of database function and chess engine.

Commercial Chess Programs

Commercial chess programs have now developed substantially over the past few years to the extent that they can now include multimedia features. The following reviews are of the leading packages

Review

Category: Chess Software: Database Program
Site Name: ChessBase
English URL: http://www.chessbase.com
German URL: http://www.chessbase.de
Spanish URL: http://www.chessbase.com/elturco/index.htm
Country: Germany
Language: English, German and Spanish

NEWS +++ NEWS +++ NEWS

FIDE threats tournament organizers
In a recent interview, Artiom Tarasov, the head of FIDE Commerce, was asked what would happen to tournaments that didn't join the GP? "In certain cases...we will organise new tournaments in the capital cities of some of these countries. This would be a slightly unfortunate situation for some events as the new Grand Prix events will be likely to take place at the same time as those events rejecting our proposal." You will find this and other stories in *John Henderson's daily column...*

Youngest GM – a Kasparov clone?
He's from Baku in Azerbaijan, he's fourteen and has just become the world's youngest grandmaster. We can be forgiven if we think Teimour Radjabov may be the result of a cloning experiment. After all isn't that exactly how (and where) it all started with Garry Kasparov? Teimour is a remarkably intelligent young boy with a disconcertingly good command of English. You can look forward to a video interview with him in ChessBase Magazine. Meanwhile you may want to read about chess prodigies throught the ages *here...*

Isn't Sashenka simply marvellous?
What possible justification could we have for presenting these racy pictures in our chess news page? Well hey, we found them on the official FIDE web site. There are more pictures and a moving story about this 16-year-old beauty *there...*

Although primarily a site for plugging products, ChessBase carries news stories

My comments

ChessBase was founded by Frederick Friedel in 1987 and was the first commercial chess database program. It came to prominence quickly due to its adoption by former World Chess Champion Garry Kasparov. Its second major product is a chess playing program called Fritz. The market for chess database systems has become very competitive but ChessBase is still the market leader, especially amongst the chess professionals. The coming of the Internet and the mass transfer of games have changed the business somewhat. It has both increased the demand for chess databases and dramatically reduced the price of raw chess games. ChessBase have noticeably concentrated on improving the look and feel of their database program, introducing multi-media elements. They have added interactive elements between their own internet site and their ChessBase program. For instance, for some time now TWIC has been available weekly as a direct one-click download from the ChessBase program (New Games). Recently they've added an on-line database of games, which can be accessed via the internet direct from ChessBase 8.

Although their website is mostly there for the promotion and support of their products, the front page does carry a number of important international news stories. They plan a whole host of new features, which will probably be ready by the time you read this book.

Products include ChessBase Magazine, with annotated games and a multi-media element (Frederick Friedel and his digital movie camera are familiar sights at many international chess events). They produce chess playing programs, the most famous of which is Fritz, but there are also championship-winning programs such as Junior. ChessBase's claim is that, although there are many sites with games, there is only one with a high quality database. Additional advice on the program can be found at http://www.chessbaseusa.com/T-NOTES/etn.htm.

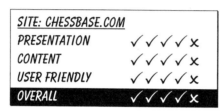

Review

Category: Chess Software: Database Program
Site Name: ChessAssistant
URL: http://www.chessassistant.com
Country: Russia
Language: English

My comments

For a brief stage in the early 1990s ChessAssistant had some claim to be the leader in database programs. Although not quite as nice to look at as ChessBase, they had a better file format, which allowed easier editing of names. They also had a chess tree that fully took into account transpositions in games.

However, they allowed their advantage to slide, while ChessBase produced a Windows version of their program and changed their limited file format to a more sophisticated one. ChessAssistant has, however, vastly improved in recent years and is still a competitive product with a loyal set of customers, both professional and amateur. It is compatible with a number of chess engines including Shredder 3 and 4, Nimzo 2000, Zarkov and Wchess (The Millennium Chess System engines – see http://www.computerchess.com). The site is a commercial one, with downloads of material and price lists, and explanation of the database and learning software.

```
SITE: CHESSASSISTANT.COM
PRESENTATION      ✓ ✓ ✓ ✗ ✗
CONTENT           ✓ ✓ ✓ ✗ ✗
USER FRIENDLY     ✓ ✓ ✓ ✗ ✗
OVERALL           ✓ ✓ ✓ ✗ ✗
```

Review

Category: Chess Software: Database Program
Site Name: Chess Academy
URL: http://www.chessacademy.de

My comments

Chess Academy is a coming name in an extremely competitive market. Their program is a combination of chess tutorial software and chess database program (with analysis engines provided). A large database is provided.

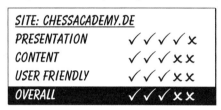

```
SITE: CHESSACADEMY.DE
PRESENTATION      ✓ ✓ ✓ ✓ ✗
CONTENT           ✓ ✓ ✓ ✗ ✗
USER FRIENDLY     ✓ ✓ ✓ ✗ ✗
OVERALL           ✓ ✓ ✓ ✗ ✗
```

Chess Computers

Whether you are a computing expert or not, the world of PC software chess playing computers can become a bit of an obsession. Here the Internet is the place to get the most up to date information and advice. There are a number of elements to a chess-playing computer. There is the interface, the opening book, table bases, and finally the chess engine.

There are commercial programs such as ChessMaster, Fritz and Rebel, but there are also free engines (some of which are incredibly strong) such as Crafty, GNU Chess, AnMon etc. There is, in fact, a division between the chess program itself and the engine that drives it. You might purchase from ChessBase a program such as Fritz or Junior, and for the price you pay you would receive a program to run engines plus the engine of your choice. So you could purchase the Junior Engine later if you bought Fritz at a lower cost, because the program to run the engine is the same.

Review

Category: Computer Chess
Site Name: Frank's Chess Page
URL: http://amateurschach.in-trier.de
Country: Germany
Language: German/English

My comments

One of the astonishing things about the Internet is the number of high quality free programs. Frank Quisinsky brings his knowledge and fascination with chess programs to a site which guides people through the world of Winboard and its compatible chess engines. The site is mainly in German but translations of key material into English make it comprehensible and allow anyone to get to the key material.

In the early days of the Internet the spirit was very much that of co-operation. People who wrote programs for their own use often made them available for general use, and more importantly, they also made the code available so that others could continue to develop the program. Xboard was a UNIX based program, which was available on the Internet in the very early 1990s, for use with a chess-playing program GNU Chess. The board was quickly developed further to allow access to the early internet servers. GNU is a special license (you can read about it at **http://www.fsf.org/copyleft/gpl.html**), which promotes co-operation and development by open computer coding. Tim Mann is the person most associated with the program after he took over its development in 1992 from the original authors. Whilst Xboard or Winboard (these are the same program – Winboard is the windows version of the program) was developed for use with GNU, chess programmers wanted to use it with their own programs and started asking Tim Mann how to do it. By stealth a protocol was developed to allow programmers to do just this (read a fascinating interview in English with Tim Mann on Frank Quisinsky's site at **http://amateurschach.in-trier.de/schach/interview/interview_tim.htm**).

Frank Quisinsky covers around 60 winboard compatible programs (45 of which are free to download and use) on this site, with information on the programmers, the program's approximate playing strength, features and links to the sites where it is available. Not only that, he also keeps track of the development of these programs.

There are two pages of overviews of each program and links to Tim Mann's overview (**http://www.research.digital.com/SRC/personal/mann/chess.html#engines**) and Volker Pittlik's overview (**http://www.ginko.de/user/volker.pittlik/schach/uebersicht2.htm**).

SITE: FRANK'S CHESS PAGE	
PRESENTATION	✓ ✓ ✗ ✗ ✗
CONTENT	✓ ✓ ✓ ✓ ✓
USER FRIENDLY	✓ ✓ ✓ ✗ ✗
OVERALL	✓ ✓ ✓ ✗ ✗

Review

Category: Computer Chess
Site Name: Tim Mann author of Winboard/Xboard
URL: http://www.research.digital.com/SRC/personal/Tim_Mann/chess.html
Country: US
Language: English

My comments

This is the official site of Tim Mann and his Winboard program. This site is defini-
tively the site where the latest release of the program is available.

Review

Category: Computer Chess
Site Name: Gambit-Soft
URL: http://www.gambitsoft.com
Country: Germany
Language: German/English

My comments

Another site that covers all sorts of chess software. Gambit-Soft is a retailer of chess
software. Nevertheless, the site has much more than that. Here's a list of their
pages: News, Chess Programs, Chess Databases, Chess Tutorials, Chess Demos,
Upgrades and Patches, Utilities, Problem Chess, PC chess boards and other material, Chess Computer Tournaments, FAQ, Pricelist, MAC programs. There are de-
scriptions and semi-reviews on the products, although you have to understand that
they are also selling these products.

The site has a single page from which you can download freeware and shareware
chess programs at **http://www.gambitsoft.com/sharee.htm**.

The site incorporates Komputer Korner at **http://www.gambitsoft.com/komputer.htm**,
which includes guides to playing on-line and to computer and database chess. Komputer Korner was the pseudonym of Alan Tomalty from Canada. He gave up and
now Harald Faber of Germany is maintaining the page.

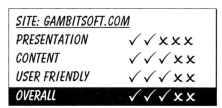

Review

Category: Computer Chess
Site Name: Chessbase Winboard Adapter
URL: http://www.chessbase.com/Products/engines/winboard/adapter.htm
Country: Germany
Language: English

My comments

Chessbase have a utility to allow winboard chess engines to run on their software.

Other useful web pages on free chess programs are:

http://azkikrs.virtualave.net/index.html – Crafty Support page. Crafty is a strong program by Bob Hyatt which is free to download. You can read about the program and how it's possible to use the code to help your own programming here.

http://cafelatte.freeservers.com/chess/index.html – How to use Crafty with Winboard.

Translations on the Internet

Within acceptable limits, it is now possible to understand an article in a foreign language via an on-line electronic translation. I believe this will be one growth area on the Internet. There has been the BabelFish translation program available on the Alta-Vista site for many years for individual web pages or short pieces of text (**http://world.altavista.com**). There is an even more effective program called teletranslator, which will continue to translate a whole site as you pass through it. It is available at **http://www.teletranslator.com**. Currently you can browse through articles in Spanish, German, Italian, Japanese or Portuguese and have them translated into English (or alternatively, articles in English translated into any of these languages). Whilst not perfect, chess generally translates pretty well and this is a huge step towards closing the language gap on the Internet.

Chapter Three

Playing on the Net

Imagine a chess club that is open 24 hours a day, 365 days a year, with players of every strength and ability. One where you have the opportunity of finding an almost unlimited number of opponents of your own ability and where you also might see a leading Grand-master turn up and play. Then welcome to the Internet, where there are many such places. My formative chess years were spent in chess clubs, playing several nights a week of competitive chess and hundreds of 5 and 10 minute blitz games. To me, there is something intensely pleasurable about moving the pieces, hitting the clock, the scramble at the end of the game when time runs short and the reaction of your opponent. The experience of playing fast chess on the Internet is quite different, but I know that for many people it's even more addictive.

If playing chess on-line can be one of the most addictive and fun parts of the Internet, it is also one of the most competitive. There are a large number of places to play chess and the choice can be at times bewildering. When I started on the Internet there was just one main place to play chess; that was on the Internet Chess Server (ICS). Many of the best sites today work in the same basic way that ICS did, still employing the same commands and ideas developed there. In those days you needed to have a basic understanding of computing to get around the Internet; certainly there was a bit of a learning curve before you could start using ICS. These days many people happily use the Internet without having a clue how to use command line operations in VT-100 terminal windows for telnet connections, and, in fact, may never have even used a DOS Window on their computer for anything. Whilst there have been graphical interfaces for playing on ICS related servers since the very early 1990's (an early example being Xboard), much of the recent effort has gone into developing these so that the player doesn't have to know any of the commands if they don't want to. These days it's possible to play on these servers being barely aware that underneath the same commands are being issued. It's a bit of a shame really, as learning to use the commands is both quicker in the long run and allows you a tremendous flexibility in the way you play chess on these servers. Whilst the ICS model serves for some servers, others use a more game-play oriented approach. On these sites, predominantly Java only, it is less complicated to set up a game but there are fewer options for each player.

Although I've played my fair share of games on-line, this isn't the main reason I have used these servers in the past. There are plenty of metaphors used to try and describe what it's like to use the Internet. People talk of surfing the Internet or cruising the Internet Highway and other such things. However, if they talk about joining the Internet Community then they may have something. There are many communities on-line, including a huge one for chess. Choosing a chess club on the Internet isn't just about the interface or ease of use (for a start they can change overnight), it's about the people you meet on-line, the quality of game you're likely to get and the general atmosphere.

The standard way of playing chess on-line is via a two-dimensional chessboard. You use a mouse to slide (another term might be pick up and drag) the pieces to the squares you want. If you want to castle, then slide the King two squares across; the server will recognise this as castling and move the rook automatically for you. If you aren't used to playing chess on a computer, then you may find that you lose quite a few games at the start by slips of the mouse. Sometimes your opponent will allow you to retract your move, especially if it's an obvious mouse-slip, but you shouldn't count on it. If you haven't played before you should just play a few games on any site without regard to result; it soon becomes quite easy to slide the pieces around the board. It is possible to enter moves manually, e.g. e4 or cxd4 etc., but almost no one finds this a good way.

I know that many people, once they find one on-line playing service, stick there forever. It is definitely worth investigating a number of different places, because this is the most popular and competitive sector of chess on the Internet. A site that is great for one person might be lousy for another. There are a number of things that you might like to take into consideration.

How many people are on-line?

Obviously, if you want a game you'd like to get on-line and get started straight away. Also you'd probably like to play a variety of opponents. You may prefer a site with relatively few regulars or a big site with a lot of players on-line. In researching this book I've even signed on to on-line playing sites with no players, which is obviously no good.

Is the site easy to use?

If you're not that computer literate, especially when you first start on the Internet, a site that is very easy to understand and use might be a priority.

Are there accounts?

It's possible to set up a chess-playing site where people log in and play but no records are kept. Most servers, however, require you to set up an account to get the best out of them. To set up an account you have to think of a nickname for yourself; this is called a called a 'handle'. You then go through the registration process with the chess server. The handle you choose might be rejected because it's already in use, so try and think of something unusual, but perhaps meaningful to you. This handle could be the only impression someone has of you, so calling yourself deathdeathchessman or sugarplumfairy might not be the image you want to convey.

You might also be asked to provide a password that you will need to remember. It's probably best to write it down. In general writing passwords down is a bad idea, but it's only on-line chess we're talking about here. Another approach is to think of a favourite book with a long title, and use the first letter of each word. An example of this approach might be *The 1,000 Best Short Games of Chess* by Irving Chernev, which could produce a password of T1BSGoCbIC. It might be that you'll be given a password at the start, but you can change it to something more memorable.

Registration is usually on-line and requires you to provide a valid email address. This check makes it slightly harder to set up multiple accounts or to return after being thrown off a server, but this is now trivial to get around. You will then automatically receive a reply with confirmation of your registration via email; this will usually occur instantly. Once you have an account set up, it means that your performances can be rated, as every time you log in using your handle and password, this acts as a check that it's you. Registered players are allowed to do more things on servers, as they are more accountable for their actions.

Are there on-line ratings?

There are two factors here. Firstly, it's quite nice to play players of your own standard and challenge yourself against harder opponents, rather than beat complete beginners. Secondly, getting that rating to go up over an evening, game by game, can be very pleasurable. Warning – ratings can go down as well as up!

Are there administrators and rules?

Bad language, abuse, cheating, sharp practice and more are a feature of real life and they are also a feature of the Internet. With administrators you can have rules. These rules can cover such things as ratings, which can be fiddled in a number of ways. If only completed games are counted, then a player who is losing may choose to disconnect to protect his record. Many places have rules against using computers during games, but people frequently succumb to the temptation to use them. It is quite possible to tell if computers are being used to help a player during a game, especially over the long run. On the more organised servers there are rules against this and administrators can enforce them. People can also inflate their ratings by getting a friend to lose lots of games to them. Or even more deviously, it's been known for players to have two accounts, one which they intend to use and another to lose games to inflate their rating on the main account.

Rules about good etiquette and behaviour can also be enforced. Administrators can help you out when you're having problems; it can be incredibly frustrating when you can't find out how to do something. These things may not be important to you if you just want a quick game every now and again, but if you start to take your on-line play seriously, or get upset when abused by an opponent (not everyone does!), then check for sites with administrators. All serious chess playing sites have administrators.

Do they run special events?

Do the chess sites run tournaments? Most of the serious sites run many events a week. They also might have lectures or demonstrate live games from grandmaster tournaments.

Choosing a Site

So where do you start? All sites will help to pair you with an available opponent and make sure the game has legal moves. There are many playing sites on the Internet. I've certainly used quite a few, although I don't spend a lot of time playing on-line at the moment.

If you were to start from scratch and search for a chess playing site, then the first two you would come across would almost certainly be two general games playing services by two of the giant concerns of the Internet. Yahoo Games includes chess at **http://games.yahoo.com/top/index.html**, as does the Microsoft gaming zone at **http://www.zone.com** and **http://www.excite.com/games/online_games**.

All services will have software that helps you find an opponent and play a legal game. They will also probably have some methods of communication, either with your opponent or with the server at large. However, it's the specialist chess sites that in my opinion offer the best chance of a good game. With administrators and on-line tournaments, as well as other events such as coverage of grandmaster tournaments and lectures from strong players, they attract people interested in chess and give better entertainment. Playing chess on Yahoo, for instance, is almost a guarantee to be abused by losing opponents. Things are slightly more civilised on Microsoft's zone.com, but they're not chess specialists and should be seen as such.

In my opinion there are four major sites for playing chess at the moment. They are the Internet Chess Club (a pay service), Free ICS, chess.net (free but with some extra services provided to people who pay) and the newcomer Kasparovchess.com. There is a pretty good case to be made to join all of them, and if you're a member of the United States Chess Federation, **http://www.uschesslive.org** can be added to the list too. Only by playing on these services and deciding what you want from a site, can an individual decide where they'd like to play the majority of their chess.

The ICC Controversy

It was a dispute that now almost seems from a different age. It was the early 1990s and the Internet was university dominated. The culture was that of co-operation and contribution. Commercialisation of the Internet was widely opposed. There were a number of telnet chess servers based on university computer systems worldwide. The most famous of these was the Internet Chess Server (ICS) based on a computer at Carnegie-Mellon University. In fact, whilst there were other servers, ICS became *the* chess server. It was the place you went to find the strongest opponents, catch up on the latest gossip and occasionally see top class grandmaster games relayed.

At the start the server was administrated by a couple of undergraduates and people from all over the World contributed to the software. Professor Daniel Sleator (in the field of computers and parsing language at Carnegie-Mellon) became involved in the autumn of 1992 and started to contribute in a small way to the programming. As the original undergraduates left he became the chief administrator (ICS handle Darooha) and over time he re-wrote the code. However, whilst previously the code had been public, now it wasn't. The server grew from 2000 members in 1993 to over 10,000 in January 1995. Over this time it became more professional. There were volunteer administrators keeping order, more features and more strong players.

In late 1994 Daniel Sleator copyrighted the name Internet Chess Server and in the first flush of the internet gold rush at that time, he received a number of offers to buy the server. He decided instead that he would, with three other partners (including Eric Peterson – another administrator), turn it into a business himself. On 1st March 1995 the Internet Chess Server had become the Internet Chess Club and the intention was to charge $49 a year to ordinary members to have accounts.

There was an angry response, both on the servers and in the internet newsgroups. The commercialisation of a previously free service provoked outrage from those who saw it as a community where people contributed not only their programming skills, but their time and ideas. People loved ICS the way it was and didn't want it to change.

Former ICS administrators and programmers such as Henrik Gram, Chris Petroff and Aviv Freidman acted almost immediately. They took the last public version of the code from two years previously, installed it on Oklahoma's State Regents for Higher Education's computer and started the Free Internet Chess Server (FICS). The coding was also rapidly improved and made publicly available. There are now a large number of servers running in different countries throughout the World.

At the time, those behind the Free Internet Server expected that the fees on the new Internet Chess Club would mean that eventually it would dwindle and die. However, ICC has survived and thrived. Free membership for Grandmasters, administrators and contributors to the original servers kept together a considerable part of the old ICS community. Subscription has meant that players on the server are well motivated; it's not a casual decision to join ICC. The atmosphere is also better than on many other servers. ICC has the strongest membership of any server worldwide and has kept its dominant position in spite of strong competition from new services. These include chess.net (which formed as a result of a breakaway from ICC by some Grandmasters, partially over a dispute over on-line advertising), the free servers and the new kasparov.com playing site.

I'm sure some would argue that ICS would have kept its dominant position without going on the commercial route. It's impossible to tell. Now there is quite a choice between different services and essentially different clubs. There is no single place to go anymore, but the growth of the Internet probably makes such a place impossible now.

What does the Internet Chess Club offer?

ICC (**http://www.chessclub.com**) is a pay service, and as such has to try and maintain itself by being better than the rest. At the moment I think it clearly is, with more of everything available: more tournaments, more live web-broadcasts, more lectures, more administrators and more titled players than everyone else. It runs using the old telnet commands (see below) that were used by ICS. After the split the telnet servers developed in slightly different ways, but the commands are all basically still the same. As such you don't get a substantially different experience on ICC than on chess.net or Free ICS. It does, however, have one of the better graphical interfaces in Blitzin, which is their recommended method of using the service. They also have different sorts of Java access, with different levels of complexity of use. It also uses Winboard (also known as Xboard), which has the merit of allowing you to connect to many different servers. You can also use one of their Java interfaces to connect to the server.

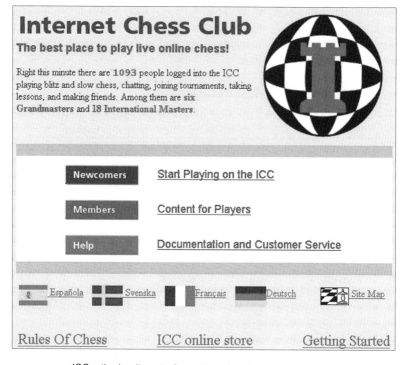

ICC – the leading site for on-line play, but you have to pay

You can get a two week free trial in order to see whether it is worth joining. I should say that I got a free account many years ago, so to me it has always remained a free service. I probably wouldn't pay for the pleasure of being a member (I really don't play enough chess on-line to justify the expense), although I do make use of its relays of international chess tournaments reasonably frequently. It provides commentaries and sometimes, especially when the official tournament site is very slow, it's useful to be able to jump in and have it as an alternative.

ICC offers free membership to Grandmasters and International Masters, which has definitely strengthened its already powerful hold as the serious players' chess site. Stars such as Alexander Grischuk, Alexander Morozevich, Alexei Dreev, Alexei Shirov, Peter Svidler, Nigel Short, Zurab Azmaiparashvili, Sergei Movsesian, Jeroen Piket and Loek Van Wely are, or have been, regulars. Garry Kasparov, Vladimir Kramnik and Viswanathan Anand have played games there in the past. Some of these Grandmasters are available for contacting, for coaching or for playing for a fee.

If you're not a titled player then it's around $50 a year, which marks it out as different from any of the other play services on the Internet. I would say that if you plan to play a lot of on-line chess, it's definitely worth joining. Otherwise, there are plenty of free alternatives which are almost as good. In the end I probably prefer ICC mostly because I have a lot of friends who play regularly there. You'll probably have to start from scratch with on-line friends, so probably any of the main servers will do.

SITE: CHESSCLUB.COM
PRESENTATION	✓ ✓ ✓ ✗ ✗
CONTENT	✓ ✓ ✓ ✗ ✗
USER FRIENDLY	✓ ✓ ✓ ✓ ✓
OVERALL	✓ ✓ ✓ ✓ ✗

Chess.net (**http://www.chess.net**) is a very similar service to ICC. There are GM lectures and transmissions of the most important tournaments. I know a number of people who find the JAVA interface easier to use than ICC, and it has built a solid following of supporters. They have pay services too, and they have a recommended graphical interface, which costs $50.

SITE: CHESS.NET
PRESENTATION	✓ ✓ ✓ ✗ ✗
CONTENT	✓ ✓ ✗ ✗ ✗
USER FRIENDLY	✓ ✓ ✓ ✓ ✓
OVERALL	✓ ✓ ✓ ✓ ✗

In the same line is the Free Internet Chess Server (**http://www.freechess.org**). They too are a popular service, with a good solid membership and some transmission of on-line chess. You can get some serious chess here if you want to.

SITE: FREECHESS.ORG
PRESENTATION	✓ ✓ ✓ ✗ ✗
CONTENT	✓ ✓ ✓ ✓ ✗
USER FRIENDLY	✓ ✓ ✓ ✓ ✓
OVERALL	✓ ✓ ✓ ✓ ✗

Kasparovchess.com is part of Garry Kasparov's mega-internet site. Whilst I am not a fan of their graphical interface, they are a free service which offer a lot of special events, including Grandmaster simultaneous displays and special challenge events you can watch. They're building a solid base of players and it's certainly worth checking out.

Graphical Interfaces

With telnet on-line playing services, the graphical interface you use will affect the way you perceive the service. There are quite a few good graphical interfaces available. Some of these have the merit of connecting you to a number of the different sites, which saves you the bother of finding them. In researching this book, I switched between servers using the freeware Xboard, which is worth having for many reasons: as a PGN reader, an interface for various free chess playing programs and a graphical interface for the various on-line services. It also runs on a number of operating systems. Xboard (**http://www.research.compaq.com/SRC/personal/mann/chess.html**) works with ICC, FICS, chess.net, and the USCF playing zone amongst others.

Another freeware board can be found at **http://www.geocities.com/TimesSquare/Alley/7007/CClientInstall.html**. There are other shareware boards (although you have to pay some registration fee after a trial period), such as SLICS (**http://www.dfong.com/chessbd/index.html**).

Blitzin (for ICC only – **http://www.chessclub.com/interface/download_sys_srv.html**) is a great graphical interface, which has plenty of help with the command set. Blitzin is free for use with ICC.

Chess.net have their own graphical interface for their service, which costs $50. It has a database and playing program (there is now a free lite version also). More details can be found at **http://www.chess.net/play/play.html**.

Kasparovchess.com also has its own graphical interface for downloading. See the prominent links on the front page at **http://www.kasparovchess.com**. It's not my favourite interface, but it may suit a beginner. You'll need either this or to use its JAVA pages to access their server.

Access to servers may increasingly be built into standard chess products. See ChessVision (**http://www.microvision.nl/default.htm**) for the way forward on this front. $70 is a bit steep for just a graphical interface, but if you like this program for its other features, it might be worth considering. The free download version also seemed to work fine as a client.

Others Playing Sites of Interest

So far we've only looked at the main chess-playing sites. Here's a list of further sites with some brief comments.

Review

Site Name: Chessed Site
URL: http://www.chessed.com

My Comments

A nice Java based site.

Review

Site Name: Vinco Online Games
URL: http://www.vog.ru

My Comments

A Russian site with some serious players.

Review

Site Name: World Chess Network
URL: http://www.worldchessnetwork.com

My Comments

Another free newcomer. They have banter chess where GMs talk about chess.

Review

Site Name: Free service to members of the United States Chess Federation
URL: http://www.uschesslive.org

My Comments

Lectures and GM exhibitions as well as tournaments. A Telnet based service that you can access not only through their software but also through Winboard.

Others

The following sites are worth an honourable mention.

Pogo.com (**http://www.pogo.com**)
On-line games site (**http://www.2am.com**)
Caissa's Web (**http://caissa.com**)
ChessWeb (**http://studwww.rug.ac.be/~mjdbruyn/chessweb**)
Achess.com (**http://www.achess.com**)
ItsYourTurn.com (**http://itsyourturn.com**)
Wireplay (**http://www.gameplay.com/wireplay**)

You could read more about playing sites at the about.com site at **http://chess.about.com/games/chess/cs/playonthenet/index.htm**.

How To Use Commands

Internet Servers via telnet are controlled by a series of commands. These cover setting up and playing the game, communication with your opponents, friends and with all the other people on the server, and customising your own settings to your needs. I've based the outline below on the instructions for ICC, but have checked them on chess.net and FICS, both of which have the same basic set of commands, as they have a common ancestor in the old Internet Chess Server. Learn for one server and you'll have a big choice of places to play on the Internet; any differences are pretty minor.

Setting up a game

We will start by looking at the commands seek, play, match, accept, decline and open. One of the easiest ways to set up a game is to use the seek command:

seek [time, increment]

For example, if you type:

seek 2 12

this translates to 'would anyone like a game of chess at a time rate of 2 minutes with an additional 12 seconds per move.'

Let's say your handle is vojo and your rating is 1835. Then your request for a game will be broadcast in the following format:

vojo (1835) seeking 2 12 rated Blitz ('play 8' to respond)

How do you receive these announcements? You have two methods. One is to change your variable for seek (more about variables later), at which point every individual seek request is sent to you ('set seek 1' for on and 'set seek 0' to not see them again). The other is the one off command 'sought', which displays all current seeks (at the time you pressed return; sometimes you have to be quick because challenges are being taken up and withdrawn quickly).

If you want to accept the challenge simply type:

play 8

and if you haven't been beaten to it by someone else, a game is automatically set up and started.

If you wish to challenge an individual player then you can send an individual request. For example, typing:

match 2 12 jimmiethefish

would challenge jimmiethefish to a game of 2 minutes with an additional 12 seconds for each move. If you receive a challenge you just type 'accept' or 'decline' (if you have more than one challenge you add the name, e.g. accept vojo if the challenge came from vojo).

If you're not interested in playing whilst you are on a server you can type 'set open 0' and this will automatically decline all challenges. You can type 'set open 1' to show you are open for them again.

You can alter things using your variables (e.g. 'set time 2' and 'set inc 12' would mean the default challenges you issue would be 2 12 games. There's also a more complicated method which gives you even more flexibility. A formula allows you to set the rating difference you'll accept, a range of time-limits, the amount of points you can lose or gain and much more. It's almost like mini-programming and uses logical operators. You should type 'help variable' if you wish to know more.

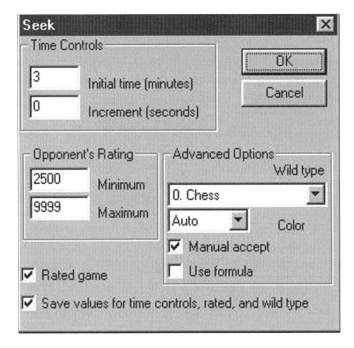

Options for 'seeking' a game on ICC

During the game

As well as playing the game and almost certainly using a graphical interface, there are a number of commands you will need to use. Here we will look at commands such as resign, flag, draw, adjourn and abort.

Obviously, the commands 'resign' and 'draw' speak for themselves. If one player offers a draw, naturally the other player has to accept or reject the offer. The software that runs the game will automatically grant a draw if it's a question of whether there's a three-fold repetition, or under the 50 move rule. The 'adjourn' and 'abort' commands ask the opponent whether they wish to do either of these and they are carried out by agreement.

There are some other commands. 'Takeback' is where you ask if you can take your last move back. Your opponent sometimes grants this if your move is an obvious blunder, usually due to a mouse-slip. With 'moretime' you can give more time to your opponent. This might be a mutual decision between the two of you, to give each other more time if you are both enjoying the game, for example, typing:

moretime 50

would give 50 seconds to your opponent.

The 'pending' command notifies you of all pending offers or draw possibilities (such as repetition or 50 move rule). 'Flag' is where you claim the game because your opponent has lost on time (if both players have no time the game is a draw). You may set a variable ('set autoflag on') which means that you automatically claim a game on time without having to issue this command. The subject of autoflag is controversial one. Some people get very upset when their flag is called and they've only just overstepped the time, especially if they suffer from a big lag (there is software called timeseal that tries to eliminate these problems by taking lag into account, but not everyone runs it). You should probably put something in your finger notes to explain your policy on this. I almost always flag, unless there is ridiculous lag or a huge unnatural gap in play, and I don't complain when flagged.

If a player disconnects during play it's usually for one of two reasons. Firstly, you should probably assume he's been disconnected from the phone; it happens quite a lot as I'm sure you know if you spend any time on the Internet. Only secondly should you assume your opponent has disconnected because he is losing. A game is adjourned automatically on disconnection of one player. If you've been disconnected you should re-connect straight away and restart the game if possible. Sometimes players refuse to restart adjourned games, and in fact, they have a lot of unfinished games; they are usually losing all of these games. Administrators will often take some sanctions against them, including awarding all of the games to their opponents, and may, in fact, change the server to always award games to their opponents when they disconnect.

Variables

Variables (some of which have been outlined above) are settings that you can change to your preference. The command 'vars' will display your own variables, while, for example, 'vars vojo' will display vojo's variables.

The command set alters variables. An example might be the 'shout' option. If you don't want to hear 'shouts' on a server, you can type 'set shout 0', or 'set shout 1' to hear them again (in most cases '0' means off and '1' means on). Some variables are about challenges and what you will and won't accept. 'Set Open 0' means that you aren't accepting any challenges for games. Type 'help vars' to see more about variables.

Below is an example list of variables for an account on ICC:

```
rated=1 wild=0 time=5 inc=0 noescape=0
minseek=0 maxseek=9999 manualaccept=0 useformula=0
open=0 ropen=1 wopen=1 ccopen=1 mood=0 seek=1 sfilter=
shout=1 sshout=1 kib=2 tell=1 ctell=1 otell=1 pin=0 gin=0 quietplay=0 tol=4
busy=0
style=12 width=78 height=18 wrap=0 prompt=1 highlight=0 bell=0
oldmatch=0 examine=0 unobserve=0 autoflag=0
who="" players="ab" lang="English"
messmail=0 automail=0 mailformat=0 addresspublic=0 namepublic=0 subscribe=0
formula = "rating > 1900"
Channels: 20 50 94 166 260
interface=""
```

Changing password

If you want to change your password, you should type

Password [Old New]

e.g., if your old password is blackpatch and your new one is greenfellow you type:

Password [blackpatch greenfellow]

Lists

There are a number of lists which are useful for administering tasks. You add items to a list by the command '+list item' and take items away by '-list item'. You can see what's in your list by typing '=list'. One example is the notify list. This is a list of friends and people of whom you want notification when they arrive on the server. Typing 'z' will list any names of players present from this list. There are other lists, such as the noplay list (players you won't play) and the alias list (basically a list of shortcuts – for instance '+alias morning shout Top of the morning to everyone!' would issue a shout of 'Top of the morning to everyone!' every time you type the command 'morning'). Then there is the censor list, which means you won't hear tells and shouts from anyone you put on this list.

Statistics

Statistics on players are recorded at the different forms of chess on the server including: blitz (less than 15 minutes per game), bughouse (a variant of chess where there are teams of two), wild (the pieces are arranged randomly at the start of the game), bullet (less than 3 minutes per game) and standard chess (more than 15 minutes per game). Typing 'finger vojo' would bring up information on the account vojo (see below). As you can see, it's my account. The information shows when you last logged on (or how long you've been on-line), the statistics, and any notes you want to make available.

If you read your own statistics you can see your name and email address, but others can't if they read them. You can make these public with the commands 'set namepublic on' and 'set addresspublic on'.

There are up to 10 lines of notes you can make for others to read. Each line is produced as follows: the command 'set 1 This is the first line of notes' would produce a first line saying 'This is the first line of notes'. You can set 0 to add notes at the end and set 11 will add a new last line of notes.

Statistics for vojo On for:2 Idle:0

	rating	[need]	win	loss	draw	total	best
Blitz	1944	[8]	50	27	8	85	2066 (14-Jan-1998)

1: Mark Crowther Editor of THE WEEK IN CHESS mdcrowth@netcomuk.co.uk

2: Interested in chess news and results.

3:

4:

5:

6:

7: THE WEEK IN CHESS http://www.chesscenter.com/twic/twic.html

The command 'history vojo' would show the most recent games played by vojo ('examine vojo 71' would show you game 71 from that player's history list). 'Logon vojo' shows the logging on history of vojo and 'vars vojo' shows the settings vojo uses for his account, including things like whether he uses autoflag.

Lag and programs to combat it

One of the main problems of playing chess over the Internet is lag. This is the amount of time that it takes for moves to be transmitted to the server from the players. So, in addition to the time you take to think over your moves and play, there is a finite amount of time associated with transmitting that move to the server. Sometimes this is so small as to be negligible, but on other occasions suddenly the game apparently grinds to a halt. If your connection is affected by lag you should take some measures, such as playing your game at a higher time increment, avoiding playing bullet (1 minute chess), asking your opponent for more time, aborting the game or adjourning the game until later. As lag tends to effect everyone at one time or another, people tend to have policies about this. You should remember that people can flag whilst you have lag and that doesn't count as bad etiquette, but many people are sympathetic. If a game has barely got started before lag hits, then many people will abort the game. Different servers also have special programs which take into account the transmission times and adjust the clocks. ICC's is called Timestamp (TM), FICS has Timeseal and chess.net has Accuclock. I believe that Kasparovchess also has a similar device too. You should check out the sites you that play on to see if such a service is available, if lag is a big and regular problem for you.

Chatting on servers

You don't have to play chess to enjoy using many of the chess servers. What better place to find people interested in chess than on a server dedicated to playing the game?

You can communicate with individuals using the command tell. For example, 'tell vojo Hi' would send the message 'Hi' to a person called vojo on the server. If you continue the conversation with the same person then you don't have to use tell. You might continue 'How are you?' and this sends the message 'How are you?' to the last person you issued a 'tell' to.

Most servers also have so called channels. These are places set up for discussion between a number of people, and places such as ICC have dedicated channels to various subjects, some not chess related. To join a channel you issue the command '+channel number', for example, '+channel 46' would put you into discussion channel 46. You can then use the tell command to communicate to everyone signed up to the channel. In this way 'tell 46 Nice weather today' would send the message 'Nice weather today' to channel 46. The command 'inchannel' lists the people in the different channels. ICC has a special channel devoted to help, which is channel 1. Requests for information can be sent there and administrators keep and eye out for queries. You should check out the individual servers to find out what each channel is devoted to.

You can communicate to the server as a whole using the command 'shout'. For example, 'shout Great Day!!!' would shout to the whole server (although you can turn off shouts by 'set shout 0'; 'set shout 1' lets you hear all shouts and on ICC 'set shout 2' restricts the shouts you hear to those of strong players and administrators). The command 'sshout' can be used for very important chess related shouts and works in the same way. You can become very irritating very quickly if you over-use the shout command; it's a good way of getting on people's censor list.

You can send messages to people's accounts with the 'message' command, for example, 'message vojo Sorry I missed you' would leave a message 'Sorry I missed you' in vojo's account for reading when he gets time. To read messages you simple type 'messages', and to get rid of them when you have read them you type 'clearmessages' (clear 1 will just get rid of message 1). During a game you can send a message to your opponent using the command 'say'; the command 'say Great Move' would send a message 'Great Move' to your opponent.

Aside from playing and chatting, you can also watch other people's games on servers. You find the number of the game that is being played and then type, for example, 'observe 27' to see game 27. If it's an interesting game there may be a few spectators watching. The command 'kibitz Great Move' would send this comment to both players and anyone watching. You can also use another command 'whisper', which only goes to those watching the game, not to the players. You can turn the kibitz command off by 'set kib 0' or restrict it to strong players by 'set kib 2'.

Who is playing?

The 'who' command lists all the players on the server at the time you issue the command, while 'games' gives a list of the games. As explained above, you can then watch games by using, for example, 'observe 3' to see game three. The command 'moves 3' would list the moves for the game. Many of the clients used for servers have special buttons for saving and collecting specific games, making this process easier.

On ICC there are libraries of games from special tournaments, for example, the 2001 twelve-game rapidplay match between Vladimir Kramnik and Peter Leko. Their games were demonstrated and placed in a file RWE2001.

Help

With all the servers there are on-line help files. Using the command 'help' on its own will give you a list basic help files and initial help. Typing 'help commands' will give additional help files and, depending on the server, may list all the commands available.

A very good introduction to ICC is available at **http://www.chessclub.com/help.html**. These commands substantially work on many other servers also.

Short cuts

Many of the commands above can be shortened to just one letter. For example 'ob 12' would work if you wanted to observer game 12. If the server doesn't have enough letters to work out which command you mean it will give a list of commands which start with that letter. The command 't vojo' works as a tell to vojo, as there are no other commands beginning with the letter t. If there are two players on the server – fredthegreat and fredsbrother – then the command 't fred' would require more clarification (unless there was a plain fred on the server, in which case the message would go to him). A shortcut of t fredt would provide just enough information to get a message to fredthegreat.

Games from the Internet

Here are some interesting blitz games played on the ICC between top Grandmasters (my thanks to John Fernandez). The first two are from the Kasparov-Svidler match on May 26, 1998. Game 1 features a nice checkmate, and game 2 a wonderful breakthrough.

In game 3, Alexander Morozevich plays some very fun sacrifices in his pet variation in the French to defeat Nigel Short, while in the final game, Alexei Shirov shows that you *can* sacrifice brilliantly against a fantastically strong computer (and get away with it).

White: Peter Svidler
Black: Garry Kasparov
Internet Chess Club Blitz 1998
Sicilian Defence

1 e4 c5 2 ♘f3 d6 3 d4 cxd4 4 ♘xd4 ♘f6 5 ♘c3 a6 6 ♗e3 e5 7 ♘b3 ♗e6 8 f3 ♘bd7 9 g4 b5 10 ♕d2 ♘b6 11 ♘a5?!

Theory gives 11 g5 as the main move here, although it's understandable that Svidler doesn't want to give away too much in an offhand blitz game. However, after this move Black gets in the crucial ...d6-d5 break and claims an early advantage.

11...b4 12 ♘e2 d5! 13 g5 ♘fd7 14 c3 bxc3 15 bxc3 ♗c5 16 ♗xc5 ♘xc5 17 ♕e3 ♕c7 18 ♘g3 0-0 19 ♘b3 ♘ca4 20 ♖c1 ♖fd8 21 ♗e2 ♘c4 22 ♕f2 ♕e7 23 h4 ♕a3 24 0-0 ♕xa2 25 ♗xc4 ♕xf2+ 26 ♖xf2 dxc4 27 ♘a5 ♖d3 28 ♘e2 ♖b8 29 ♘c6 ♖b5 30 ♘b4 ♖d6 31 f4 exf4 32 ♘xf4 ♘xc3 33 e5 ♖d4 34 ♘xe6 ♖g4+ 35 ♔f1

♖xb4 36 ♘d8 ♖d5 37 ♖xf7 c3 38 ♖d7 ♖bf4+ 39 ♔e2 ♖g2+ 40 ♔d3

This allows Black a nice mate, although 40 ♔e1 is also losing after 40...♖e4+ 41 ♔f1 ♘e3+ 42 ♔e1 ♖xh4.

40...♖d2 mate (0-1)

White: Garry Kasparov
Black: Peter Svidler
Internet Chess Club Blitz 1998
Ruy Lopez

1 e4 e5 2 ♘f3 ♘c6 3 ♗b5 a6 4 ♗a4 ♘f6 5 0-0 ♗e7 6 ♗xc6

Once again we see a desire to stay clear of the most critical lines, although Kasparov has used this quiet line of the Ruy Lopez once or twice in serious games.
6...dxc6 7 d3 ♘d7 8 b3 c5

8...0-0 9 ♗b2 f6 10 ♘bd2 ♘c5 11 d4! exd4 12 ♘xd4 led to a plus for White in Kasparov-Beliavsky, Reykjavik 1988.
9 ♗b2 ♗d6 10 ♘bd2 0-0 11 ♘c4 f6 12 ♘h4 ♘b8 13 ♘f5 ♗xf5 14 exf5 ♘c6 15 ♕f3 ♕d7 16 ♕e4 ♔h8 17 ♖fe1 b5 18 ♘e3 ♘d4 19 c3 ♘c6 20 ♖ad1 ♖ad8 21 h4 ♖fe8 22 h5 h6 23 g3 ♘e7 24 g4 c6 25 c4 ♗b8 26 ♘g2 ♕b7 27 ♘h4 ♖d7

White has a space advantage, but further progress is difficult due to the blocked nature of the position.

28 ♘g6+ ♔g8 29 f4 ♘xg6 30 fxg6 ♖de7 31 f5 ♖d7 32 ♗c3 ♖ed8 33 ♔f1 ♗c7 34 ♖e3 ♗b6 35 ♖f3 ♕c7 36 ♔g2 ♖d6 37 ♖h3 ♖8d7 38 g5!

Destroying Black's blockade.

38...♗a5 39 ♗b2 ♕d8 40 gxh6 gxh6 41 ♕e3 bxc4 42 bxc4 ♕b8 43 ♗a3 ♗b4 44 ♗c1 ♗c3 45 ♕e2 ♔g7 46 ♕c2 ♕b4 47 ♔h1 ♕a5

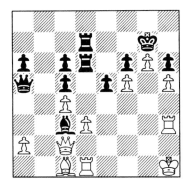

48 ♗xh6+!

This breakthrough leads to a forced win. **48...♔xh6 49 ♕c1+ ♔g7 50 h6+ ♔h8 51 g7+ ♔h7 52 ♖g1 ♖d8 53 g8♕+ ♖xg8 54 ♖g7+ 1-0**

White forces checkmate after both 54...♖xg7 55 hxg7+ ♔xg7 56 ♕h6+ ♔f7 57 ♕g6+ ♔e7 58 ♖h7+ ♔d8 59 ♕g8 mate and 54...♔h8 55 ♕g1 ♖dd8 56 ♕g6.

White: Nigel Short
Black: Alexander Morozevich
Internet Chess Club Blitz 1999
French Defence

1 e4 e6 2 d4 d5 3 ♘d2 ♗e7

A slightly offbeat line, which has been popularised of late by both Morozevich and Short.

4 ♗d3 c5 5 dxc5 ♘f6 6 ♕e2 dxe4 7 ♘xe4 ♘xe4 8 ♗xe4 0-0 9 ♘f3 ♘d7!?

9...♗xc5 keeps the material balance, but the time control encourages Morozevich to be adventurous.

10 c6 bxc6 11 ♗xc6 ♘c5!? 12 ♗xa8 ♗a6 13 ♕e5

13 c4 ♘d3+ 14 ♔f1 ♗xc4 keeps White under pressure. Objectively it's unclear how good Black's sacrifice is, but in a blitz game it's extremely difficult for White to keep things under control

13...♕xa8 14 ♗e3 ♖c8 15 ♕f4 ♕b7 16 ♗xc5

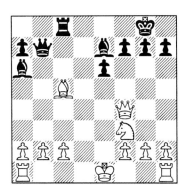

16...♕xb2! 17 ♕e5

17 ♗xe7 allows 17...♕xa1+ 18 ♔d2 ♕c3+ and Black mates.

17...♕xe5+ 18 ♘xe5 ♖xc5 19 ♘d3 ♖xc2 20 ♖d1 ♖xa2 21 0-0 ♖a3 0-1

Black wins back the exchange and remains two pawns up.

White: Alexei Shirov
Black: Ferret
Internet Chess Club Blitz 1996
Giuoco Piano

1 e4 e5 2 ♘f3 ♘c6 3 ♗c4 ♗c5 4 d3 ♘f6 5 c3 a6 6 ♘bd2 d6 7 ♗b3 0-0 8 0-0 ♗a7 9 ♖e1 ♗e6 10 ♗c2?

This allows Black to win material, and typically the computer is not slow to seize its chance.

10...♘g4 11 ♖e2 ♗xf2+! 12 ♖xf2 ♘e3 13 ♕e2 ♘xc2 14 ♖b1 ♗xa2 15 b3 ♗xb1 16 ♘xb1 ♘a1 17 ♕b2 d5 18 ♘bd2 dxe4 19 dxe4 ♘xb3 20 ♕xb3

With a rook and three pawns for two minor pieces, Black should have some advantage, but...

20...b5 21 h4 ♕d7 22 ♗a3 ♖fe8 23 ♘g5 ♘d8 24 ♘df3 c6 25 ♖d2 ♕a7+ 26 ♔h2 a5 27 ♕d1 h6 28 ♖d7 ♕e3 29 ♗e7 hxg5 30 ♗xg5

Surely this sacrifice cannot work against a strong computer?

30...♕b6 31 h5 ♘e6 32 h6 ♘c5 33 hxg7 ♘xd7 34 ♘h4

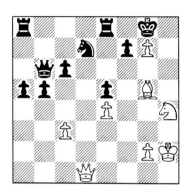

34...♕c7?

34...c5 is correct, although after 35 ♕h5 f6 36 ♗e3 White still has a strong attack.

35 ♕h5!

Now it's forced mate

35...f6 36 ♘f5 ♕b6

Or 36...fxg5 37 ♕g6, followed by ♘h6 mate.

37 ♕g6 ♕g1+ 38 ♔xg1 fxg5 39 ♘h6 mate (1-0)

Chapter Four

News and Events

I make my living by reporting on the sporting aspects of chess on my web page *The Week in Chess* (TWIC – **http://www.chesscenter.com/twic/twic.html**).

HOME | TWIC | SHOP | EVENTS | BRIDGE

Feedback for news sections
Write to Mark Crowther: E-Mail-mdcrowth@netcomuk.co.uk

Last update 09-30 GMT 04-30 EST Wednesday 28th March 2001.

TWIC Weekly Digest of Chess News: Last issue TWIC 333 26th March 2001| ChessPublishing | Book Reviews by John Watson | PAST TWIC ISSUES | Henderson reports | Obituaries | Fantasy Chess League | Important Events of 2000 | Important Events of 2001

- **Main news stories**
- Kasparov won the World Cup of Rapid Chess when he beat Evgeny Bareev in the final 1.5-0.5 when Bareev resigned game two with only a few seconds left in what appears very much to be a drawn position. (44. ...Kc6 45.Kc4 Kd6 46.Kb5 Kd5 47.Kxa5 Ke4 48.a4 Kxf4 49.Kb6 Kg3 50.a5 f4 51.a6 f3 52.a7 f2 53.a8Q f1Q is equal).
- New Amber tournament round 8.
- Latest John Watson Book review of 27th March 2001. Review #34 A Remarkable Publisher and Other Topics
- China beat US 21-19 John Henderson's Round 4 report US-China Chess Summit Match
- Linares final results. Kasparov 7.5 everyone else 4.5.

The Week in Chess – my own contribution to chess on the net

The results, the games and the stories surrounding the top players are amongst the great highlights of chess on the Internet. This is one of the most well covered areas and live transmission of the elite tournaments is now the norm. The competitiveness has also led to an increase in extras, such as reports, pictures and even live web television coverage. In less than ten years we have gone from being pathetically grateful for any scraps of information and games we could get, to the expansive completeness we have now. I also believe that things will get even better as bandwidth on the Internet continues to grow. Chess is ideally suited to the internet age. Whilst it is perceived as a minority sport in some ways, internationally there is a potentially large audience for the right event.

Sites reporting chess news fall into many categories. They may like my page TWIC (which for better or worse has proved a model for many having been around so long), in that they report the main news stories, give games and link to the major events of the week. Pages similar to mine appear in many languages worldwide and if you know what you're looking for you can navigate your way round sites without understanding the language. You can also run many of these sites through translation software such as Alta Vista's Babel Fish site (**http://world.altavista.com**) or **http://teletranslation.com**.

Other sites have a specific focus: they may cover the most major international chess events in their own language but they concentrate on covering events in their own country or part of the world. This is also another division: some sites scour the Internet for information; others actually are the source of the stories or games. These could be sites of chess federations or of leading national chess magazines. There are sites, such as Lost Boys, who are companies that specialise in providing electronic boards to the major international events. They also provide the web coverage for those events. Then there is the International Chess Federation's (FIDE's) site, which has gone through a number of incarnations in recent years. It is the source for information about the federation, live coverage of its own events and international ratings. This site now appears under the control of FIDE Commerce, a separate organisation. With changes within FIDE this page is likely to become more important in the coming years.

Sites belonging to individual players can give a personal view of an individual event, perhaps with some annotated games. Kasparovchess.com falls into a special category. From a news point of view, its greatest importance is in the access it has to Kasparov, who freely gives interviews and commentary. They have also staged their own events and had the budget to provide detailed coverage of the most important events. In fact, Kasparovchess.com had a huge budget in the first year, but will probably continue with less of an advantage in this area in the future, at least until a stock market flotation can be organised.

Many of the chess servers relay the moves from major chess tournaments. ICC has its own quite detailed library of such news and events. A number of rivals do similar things; they also bring in top players for on-line question and answer sessions.

How TWIC is Compiled

Almost every week since September 1994 I have produced an internet chess magazine called *The Week in Chess*. Throughout 1993 and 1994 I posted news stories and games I had collected from newspapers and magazines to the newsgroups. In September 1994 I decided that doing this every day was taking up a lot of time. Instead I decided that on a Saturday morning I would collect the stories and the most important games and put them in one place. I found rather quickly that this didn't really save me the time I had anticipated. I was sent news and games from chess journalists who used TWIC, so in only a few months I actually ended up with far more material than had been seen on the Internet before.

I've always enjoyed the elite chess tournaments; getting news stories and all the games from these events was my original idea. Nevertheless, I couldn't really turn down lesser events that people had taken the time and effort to send me. Each issue of the magazine typically had around 14 news stories and several hundred games in PGN. The complexity and volume of material I had to deal with quickly turned my task from a morning hobby to something that took me Friday night, Saturday morning and Sunday night to compile, all my free weekend time away from work. Something had to give, and by 1996 I decided I either had to find a sponsor full time or cut back considerably.

In August 1996 I signed up with Thoth, which was part of Grandmaster Technologies (GM Tech) and left my job at Bradford University. At the time of the 100th issue of TWIC I commented that since I started the magazine, just two years before, things had changed massively; it was now inconceivable that a major event would not be covered on the Internet by the organisers. At the time the FIDE Olympiad went ahead with its first full internet coverage (I'd had to beg for some games from the database company ChessAssistant two years earlier).

A year later GM Tech started to run out of money and I had to find another sponsor. The magazine continued on their site for three months before I found my current sponsor in December 1997 and moved to the London Chess Centre's site at **http://www.chesscenter.com/twic/twic.html**.

When I worked at Bradford University I used their UNIX computer system. I didn't have a database at the time, so completeness (some people want every game they can lay their hands on), consistency (are the names of the players in exactly the same form between tournaments; for example is it Korchnoi, Kortchnoi or Korchnoij and is it V, Victor or Viktor?) and the ratings of players in the games sections were not an immediate issue for me. Around a year after starting I began to do some serious work on the games sections.

In 1994 Anjo Anjewierden had started developing a series of programs and utilities to help both with historic tournaments and current ones. One of these was called cutour (his homepage is at **http://www.anjo.demon.nl**). This program, to which he was kind enough to add features at my request, takes games in old ChessBase format and processes the games into PGN. This was a huge step in improving the quality of the games in TWIC, but it also meant the magazine took far longer to compile. Once you start working on games it really becomes a job, not a hobby.

Cutour reads a file called players.ppn, which has a host of information about every FIDE rated player in the world; if it recognises a player's name it adds the rating to that player. It's not the easiest program to use and it can introduce errors when it falsely recognises a player who turns out to be someone different (for instance Regina and Renata Pokorna, who are sisters; Regina is the younger sister but she is stronger and plays much more chess than her sister).

One of the aspects of PGN standard that is widely ignored is over naming. The standard says 'The format used in the FIDE rating lists is appropriate for use for player name tags.' For a time this proved a little hard to stick to, as the most widely used database format was ChessBase. Its format, which had been around since the 1980s, had only limited space for the names of players. If names were too long, all sorts of effects could happen, including the loss of round numbers. Cutour uses a shortened form of names, with the first name cut down to its minimum. For instance, in the case of Julian Hodgson it is 'Hodgson, Ju', to differentiate him from 'Hodgson, Jo', which is an abbreviation of John Hodgson, a completely different player. I've continued using this short form, although it's now been rendered unnecessary with the change in ChessBase format starting with ChessBase 6.

I stick to the naming convention used in the FIDE list, with the above proviso. The reason for this is, even though there are errors in the FIDE list (even Kasparov's name is wrong; many years ago he decided on the spelling Garry rather than Gary, but it's never been changed), the list does at least give everyone a chance at consistency if they choose to use it (the full FIDE list is available a **http://www.fide.com** in the ratings section).

It's especially important for double-barrelled names such as Ivan Morovic Fernandez, which is frequently given as Ivan Morovic. This can lead to multiple spellings across single tournaments, never mind different ones. There are also special problems created by people with the same name, such as Andres Rodriguez (one from Spain, who hardly plays at all: another from Uruguay, a GM, who plays a lot). I use the name 'Rodriguez, And URU' for the common one. If 'Rodriguez, A' is given in a database, you have to work out not only which of eleven players this might be in the rating list (there are also two Albertos) but also whether it might be one of another five players who have names such as Rodriguez Vinuesa or Rodriguez Azahara).

Cutour also fills in the other information required by the PGN format, such as country, event and date information. It is certainly not the only way to do things; it's very possible to achieve many of these tasks in top of the range programs such as ChessBase and Chess Assistant. However, if you're publishing games of a tournament on the Internet you should use some tools to straighten out the names and the event and carry out some small checks on the material. It's likely to find its way into a lot of databases in whatever state you leave it in.

The Internet is awash with games. It's never been my intention to be complete, except for top events. Once players drop below my level of play (around 2100 ELO as an estimate) it's an open question as to whether I need to publish them in TWIC; I've never considered my games as being worthy of publication. You can find collections of millions of games on the Internet. If you want them to study your opening repertoire or to look at whether a move has been played before, they're great. If you've never had access to significant quantities of games before you'll find it an unbelievable resource. Do remember, however, that these game collections are full of errors. There are mistakes everywhere: in results, players' names, moves, as well as omission of details such as dates and round numbers;

almost anything is possible. Even at the elite level I would say that a minimum 20% of games given on the Internet are significantly flawed in some way or another, perhaps even 40%. Thankfully, the more important an event, the more likely they will be correct.

Reasons for mistakes include poor or no pay for entering games (I've typed in my share of games over the years; it's not one of the World's most exciting or rewarding tasks), or blind faith in electronic boards (they're great but they introduce a lot of errors too, especially if the operators are overburdened or just inexperienced). It would be great if a little care was taken at source before games are sent out; once an incorrect version acquires any significant distribution the right and wrong version will remain in cyberspace forever.

I've come to admire the work of some websites and people who have very exacting standards, such as John Saunders (who eventually graduated from the Internet and became editor of *British Chess Magazine*); it's a pleasure to see work done well.

For TWIC I produce games sections with typically 350 to around 1500 games a week; they're not perfect but they're often a significant improvement over the originals and I do correct games that are drawn to my attention.

Another way of getting games into a usable condition is to use a text editor (I use textpad **http://www.textpad.com**, which is a great program). A long time ago I was told by an American called Elliott Winslow to think things out and find the best method of doing things using a computer, as it will save time in the long run. I now use macros (a little script which repeats the same process throughout a file) to solve a lot of common problems which I used to do by hand. If you get a PGN file of games with no round numbers you can use 'search and replace'. If they have no commas between names you can put them in manually or, if you think things out, using a macro (the same goes for files of games where the names are all in capital letters). It's possible to lick almost any rubbish into shape with a combination of a text editor and a database such as ChessBase or Chess Assistant (these both have libraries which allow you to normalise names).

Sometimes I'm sent games that aren't in a database format but in a text format: a little header at the top and then the games. The rule here is if you can make it look like PGN it will probably work as PGN. That is, you edit the headers so that the names and details are in PGN format, perhaps adding the results using a utility such as Normal32.exe (available at the U4Chess Page by Paul Onstad – **http://www.sihope.com/~ponstad**).

Sometimes you get files that are not in English. Here you have to turn the moves into English first by 'search and replace'. Make sure you make the search case sensitive, that is, search for capital letters (this can have a big effect on the names of the players that have to be sorted out later). You also have to watch for the use of R for King in some languages (for example in Spanish), making sure you change R to K before you change T to R. With practice you can convert huge text files into usable PGN this way.

You also find out if people have typed games in 'freehand'. When I started on the Internet I used to try and type games in from newspapers by simply copying the text. Only the most exceptional person can get this right and I have a great respect for those who had to do this before the age of computers. There are typical errors introduced to game scores, such as moving the wrong rook or knight to a square.

English	P	N	B	R	Q	K
Czech	P	J	S	V	D	K
Danish	B	S	L	T	D	K
Dutch	O	P	L	T	D	K
Estonian	P	R	O	V	L	K
Finnish	P	R	L	T	D	K
French	P	C	F	T	D	R
German	B	S	L	T	D	K
Hungarian	G	H	F	B	V	K
Icelandic	P	R	B	H	D	K
Italian	P	C	A	T	D	R
Norwegian	B	S	L	T	D	K
Polish	P	S	G	W	H	K
Portuguese	P	C	B	T	D	R
Romanian	P	C	N	T	D	R
Spanish	P	C	A	T	D	R
Swedish	B	S	L	T	D	K

Chess piece letters from different countries

There are many free software and database programs you can use for entering games; make use of them. This method will give you legal moves and much more accuracy. Most of the time you'll pick up errors you've made because some moves you try to make later on will become impossible, due to these same errors earlier in the game. I've been through files of games typed in freehand; three or four error moves per game is typical, where it's not clear which rook or knight has gone to a square, or errors on the players score sheet are repeated.

A few days before Monday I start to plan what's going to be in the TWIC magazine. I'm sent a lot of material by email, which I will start to go through. There will be a number of different types of article to choose from.

Event Reports and Results

In the event of games, I have to look at how long it is likely to take me to sort the names out. Olympiads are amongst the hardest, with so many players, some of whom are not ELO rated. In fact any event with a mixture of rated and non-rated players can be tough.

Are the events complete? It's possible to check the results given by the games and the official results if the games from an event are complete. In the case of all-play-all tournaments it's possible to check whether all the players' names and round numbers are correct. If there are mistakes then cutour picks them up. There's a draw for the pairings at the start of an all-play-all event and it's possible to calculate what the draw for the whole event should be from any two rounds. Processing the games is the single most time consuming thing I do. I like to do this; it's what separates TWIC from most other sites.

Interviews, Press releases and Letters

You have to be careful with copyright material but I link to important interviews and publish some material from important press releases. Occasionally I get letters from GMs wanting to air one subject or another.

If I have time, I might comment on some aspect of the news. It should be said, however, that the controversial subjects tend to be the same (Kasparov and FIDE in one way or another and there is only so much you can say). Since 1994 chess players have had a very good idea what goes on during a FIDE Congress, whether that's actually helped is open to question.

With my sponsorship agreement I also keep the main page of TWIC stocked with links and tournament coverage, I always like to put at least some stories in my magazine, but not on the front page. Also the London Chess Centre has in recent times sent correspondents to major tournaments. Its main correspondent is John Henderson, who also takes pictures in addition to filing reports. As well as this we've covered events that have been hosted on our site with live coverage. In addition writers have contributed to the front page; there's John Watson's highly respected book reviews and Michael Greengard's (Mig's) reports on major tournaments (he went on to get a high profile job in charge of content at Kasparovchess.com).

Live Coverage of Games

Everyone has a different idea of how this should be done properly. In the early 1990s matches such as Fischer-Spassky in 1992 and Kasparov-Short in 1993 saw the use of finger sources similar to the ones you can still see on online chess sites such as ICC and FICS. All you had to do was to type 'finger <email address>' and this brought up a few lines of text, perfect for a single game of chess. Since then there have been multiple methods of reporting games, but I certainly wonder if they've been a great improvement in some areas.

If you are sponsoring or running a major international chess event, internet coverage is now a big part of that. Live coverage brings big hits and obviously companies appreciate this. A large number of the hits, however, will be from the same people pressing 'reload' to get the latest moves. This can bring down even the largest and most sophisticated servers; during the final match between Kasparov and IBMs Deep Blue even IBM struggled with the load.

Important factors

If the event is going to be major international interest you have to ask the question, 'Will my server be able to cope?' If you've invited many top players then you need to be very sure of your computing power. Without specific agreement with your service provider you might even find your coverage cut off. Whereas hits per se don't mean very much to advertisers these days (it's the number of visitors and page impressions), they do mean a great deal to your service provider. It needs more power for more hits and you may be cut off if you overload the system (or indeed the system might seize up anyway). The website for the 2000 Sarajevo tournament almost lacked sufficient power to cope with the hits. If you suspect that this is going to be the case then simple coverage with PGN or just the moves in text may be a solution.

Will you cover the tournament live, at the end of play, or distribute the moves to news sites that are more than grateful to have them? It's down to the resources you can put into internet coverage. When an important tournament is on people reload your page many times; if they're waiting for a key move in a game it could be many times a minute. This produces highly unusual loads for chess servers to cope with.

Whatever flashy presentation you use on your site you should always have the basics. These include:

1) Clear summaries of the results and current standings, kept up to date, ideally during play for major all-play-all tournaments.

2) The dates and times of the event and any rest days during it.

3) Games in PGN; these should have the correct round numbers and dates. Don't put each game in a separate PGN file either. Keep at least each round together in a single file.

Once you have provided those basics you can think of elements that are optional:

1) Photos, reports and annotations.

2) Players comments and interviews.

3) Webcams and chat.

Keep to these and you have a functional site that is easy to use. Just ask yourself the question, 'Would I find the site welcoming if I visited it?' So many sites seem almost designed to hide information and make its retrieval difficult. Keep the site light on graphics if you expect a lot of hits and lack the computing power to cope.

Transmitting moves

How will you transmit the moves? There are a number of commercial companies that specialise in live coverage of major international events. They are brought in by the organisers to provide the coverage both on the Internet and in the tournament hall itself.

In recent years the leading company seems to be Lost Boys, who cover leading events such as Wijk aan Zee and the Frankfurt Chess Classic rapidplay. Their site is at

http://chess.lostcity.nl and their parent company's site is at **http://www.lostboys.com**. Their coverage involves a Java viewer for all the games. This is an html format, which also serves a form of PGN and allows you to choose the games you want to update. Also included in their coverage are reports, chat and a webcam.

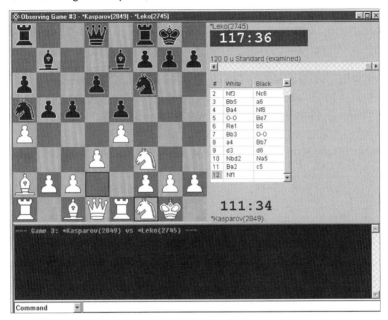

Kasparov v Leko, Linares 2001 live on the ICC site

Another Dutch company called TASC (**http://www.tasc.nl**) was for many years the leading company, but it hasn't covered many events recently. They offer live html, Java and html viewers and reports.

Major Spanish events tend to be covered by Ajedrez21 (**http://www.ajedrez21.com**). This site has had a number of different names over the years but it's the same people. An example of the kind of event they do would be the Linares super-GM tournament. They allow options of viewing with html (where you see a single game) and Java viewer (all games), some video stills and a chat channel.

FIDE (**http://www.fide.com**) cover their own events and have their own display system that they have used for a couple of years now. At the start of events they have had problems getting the electronic boards to work properly, but they almost always get the moves delivered well after two or three rounds. I do, however, have a problem with the method they use to transmit games to the Internet. The interface looks nice and works reasonably effectively for small events. The problem as far as I'm concerned is that FIDE events are usually huge. Every two years there is the Olympiad, which is the single largest chess event there is, and of course there is the FIDE World Championships, which that will start with 128 players from now on. The FIDE website only displays one game in its Java viewer. To reach any single game you have to travel a tortuous path to get there, then go back and forward again to reach another game, each stage being quite slow to execute.

As well as this, to follow a game live I like to check the positions in a database, perhaps using a playing program for general assessment. The Java viewer doesn't give you the game score in a usable form (although sometimes it's possible to download the files they use to power the viewer). The advent of FIDE Commerce means that they will probably cover more events in the future, so it is to be hoped this aspect improves.

FIDE already have a better model for covering their events. The 1st FIDE World Cup took place in Shenyang, China in 2000 (**http://www.worldchesscup.com**). Their live coverage was very simple, a zipped PGN file which was viewable using MyChess Viewer 2.1 by Michael Keating. I feel this was technically one of the best and most effective methods of transmitting moves, and it kept me watching the games.

There is a Russian company called Shahcom (**http://www.ruschess.com**) who also provide commercial electronic live coverage.

Do it Yourself

If an event is of a lower profile, which makes bringing in professional help prohibitive, then it is possible to produce live coverage or semi-live coverage yourself.

There are electronic chessboards available for purchase. The DGT Fritz board, along with Lost Boys software, can be used for live broadcasts. A number of specialist shops sell it and you can read more about DGT at **http://www.dgtprojects.com**. It does require some skill and practice to use and can be a bit clunky. If you use the Lost Boys software make sure a PGN file is available (this is an option). At the 2000 Sarajevo event, won by Garry Kasparov, the tournament was hosted by the Bosnia Government's Sarajevo City site at **http://www.ks.gov.ba**. The level of interest was such that communication was extremely slow. They used the electronic board and a demonstration in html (no PGN), and many times only half the page loaded. A PGN option would have been smaller and would have reduced the load on the site significantly.

At the end of play, if you are using electronic boards, you must check the game over against the players' score sheets. There are often problems, including extraneous moves at the end of the game, or positions where a piece slid along the board and a number of extra moves are introduced; these all should be resolved as quickly as possible.

Of course you don't need to use an electronic board at all. For most of the last century major tournaments have had demonstration boards updated by runners watching the games. These moves can be entered into a database and then transmitted to the Internet. ChessBase and ChessAssistant have features that allow you to produce html pages. Again, along with these, you should also include the ability to download a PGN file.

There are also Java viewers for PGN files. The problems associated with Java viewers are many: they don't work on some browsers and also they can tax the system resources of many computers. I run into problems with many of them when I run a few other programs (say ChessBase, an html editor and a couple of other browser windows). Nevertheless, they are very useful for the casual watcher of games who don't have their own programs to read PGN. A Java viewer is an option that should be provided. There are a number of free game demonstrators on the Internet.

As mentioned before, I was impressed with the functionality of the MyChess Java viewer. MyChess, by Michael Keating (**http://www.mychess.com**), seems light on system resources and reloads from either a PGN file or a zipped PGN file. This also means that users can have the option of downloading these files too. If there's no specific link you can check the source code for the viewer and see where it is accessing the games from, while a zipped PGN file can be very quick to reload. It isn't a very aesthetic viewer (the nicest in appearance is the one used by Lost Boys), but its functionality impresses me greatly.

There are other good and free alternatives. TWIC has used at times the Chess Tutor Java viewer, which allows you to set up links to multiple files. You can read all about it at the author's (Eduardo Suastegui's) website **http://members.nbci.com/esuastegui/eschess**.

There is also the Misty Beach PGN Java viewer. Read more at **http://www.mistybeach.com/products/PGNViewer**.

Another alternative, similar to the approach used by ChessBase, is Javascript. Javascript is completely different from Java – Java is a program, Javascript is an enhanced form of html. Palview is a PGN to HTML conversion utility by Andrew Templeton. You can read about and download it at **http://www.cowderoy.com/chess/palview**.

Where to Find News

There are a huge number of internet sites that carry chess news and links to news stories. They are generally a mix of news from the host country (which may be original source material) and the most important international events. These sites can be written by chess enthusiasts, have a promotional aspect for a printed chess magazine or publisher, be a site for chess software or for a bookshop. It might be a chess federation's site or have any number of other reasons for existing. As TWIC has been around for so long I am lucky in that I'm sent many of the news stories and links by their originators, but there is always a news story or tournament that I miss out on. If you limit yourself to one language in this area you will miss out. With translation programs available between many languages, and with a little common sense, you can certainly widen the number of places you can visit and appreciate.

I compiled a list of over 90 sites which I categorised as chess news, many of which are good. This didn't include other sites which were magazines, database supplies or a mixture. I've had good relations with many of the webmasters over the years so I don't upset too many people, but space is limited here. I will leave out many worthwhile sites in these reviews and the accent will be on sites which link to others and are written in English or easily understood in any language.

On the front page of TWIC (**http://www.chesscenter.com/twic/twic.html**) I place the latest news stories and links. It's worth checking the French site Notzai (**http://www.notzai.com**) as they pick up very quickly on timely links to events worldwide and present them very clearly, with a daily summary of the most important places to go. Then I would also check out **http://www.Kasparovchess.com** for any news stories and especially interviews. They only go to town on a limited number of events a year, but when they do the coverage is very good. You can also take in the Chesswatch part of the site, which rounds up some links you may not have seen.

♛ Kasparov Express

Express Commentary by Garry Kasparov: Round 4
A young star is turned back

By Garry Kasparov

Finally I've opened the scoring in Linares! Today I can say that both the result and the quality of the game were satisfactory. I applied a new idea in a topical variation of Sicilian: Black was going to round up his opponent's knight stuck on a4. Grischuk correctly traded queens and we passed to a complicated position with mutual chances. Let's see...
1.e4 c5 2.Nf3 d6 3.d4 cxd4 4.Nxd4 Nf6 5.Nc3 a6 6.f3 Qb6 7.Nb3 e6 8.Qe2 Qc7 9.g4 b5 10.Be3 b4 11.Na4 Nbd7 12.Qc4
Otherwise Black is better:
- 12.g5? Nxe4 13.fxe4 Qc6;
- 12.Qd2 Rb8
12...Qxc4 13.Bxc4 d5 Just in time. **14.exd5 Ne5 15.Be2 Nxd5 16.Bd4 Bd6**
This is the end of home preparation. I considered this position to be quite promising for Black, so I went for it willingly - but one can hardly affirm that Black has advantage here. White's K-side looks ugly (as they say, g4-g3 is the best move here but, alas, pawns can't go backwards!) but Black is still a bit behind in development.

KasparovChess often features instant notes from the man himself

SITE: KASPAROVCHESS.COM
PRESENTATION ✓✓✓✗✗
CONTENT ✓✓✓✓✓
USER FRIENDLY ✓✓✓✗✗
OVERALL ✓✓✓✓✗

NetChessNews (**http://www.httpcity.com/ncn**) has an idiosyncratic look at the latest news, concentrating on the top news stories, games and then perhaps a couple of less obvious stories. **http://www.chesslines.com**, a French site that is also in English, seems to be becoming quite active now. The FIDE site **http://www.fide.com** has essential information such as ratings, and its press releases section is important, often containing quite big stories. This is the place to find live games from its own events also.

SITE: FIDE.COM
PRESENTATION ✓✓✓✓✗
CONTENT ✓✓✓✓✗
USER FRIENDLY ✓✓✓✗✗
OVERALL ✓✓✓✓✗

If you're interested in chess in Germany then **http://www.schach.com** is a good place for news and links, especially for events such as the super-strong German Bundesliga. **http://www.chessgate.de** is a new site which may develop further (it provided the internet coverage for a match between Kramnik and Leko at the start of 2001 and also has commented on games from other events).

For events in Britain and major chess tournaments there is the British Chess Magazine site **http://www.bcmchess.co.uk**.

```
SITE: BCMCHESS.CO.UK
PRESENTATION      ✓ ✓ ✓ ✓ ✗
CONTENT           ✓ ✓ ✓ ✓ ✗
USER FRIENDLY     ✓ ✓ ✓ ✓ ✗
OVERALL           ✓ ✓ ✓ ✓ ✗
```

The ChessBase site **http://www.chessbase.com** also carries some exclusive stories and I hear it has plans to expand its new service. Another fertile place to find breaking news is in the newsgroup rec.games.chess.misc. For live coverage of some of the major events you could also check out the on-line server ICC (**http://www.chessclub.com**). Another site to check out is the Canalweb site. This French site has pioneered the use of Web TV in the coverage of chess. Their finest hour was the live coverage of the Brain Games World Chess Championships, but they have made programs on many of the best events over the last couple of years. Their site is at **http://www.canalweb.com** and is in French. You need to follow links for Jeux and then Echecs (Games and then Chess) to find the latest programs.

Another place to go daily is the Spanish newspaper *El Pais*. Spain is a very important place in international chess and *El Pais*' chess correspondent Leontxo Garcia gets a lot of good stories. Click on the Deportes (sport section) and find the Ajedrez section. The past seven days' papers are available at **http://www.elpais.es/sietedia.htm** and teletranslator.com can be used to make a very acceptable translation. Another important columnist is Arvind Aaron of *The Hindu* (**http://www.the-hindu.com**). If you go to the sports section you can read his chess articles. India is experiencing an upswing in interest in chess and there is chess news available almost daily. Aaron frequently travels to major events involving FIDE World Champion Viswanathan Anand. Another worth looking at is **http://www.chathurangam.com**, which is an excellent site concentrating on Indian chess, but with an international view, especially when Anand is playing.

In the United States there are only a few sites with news from that region. **http://www.insidechess.com** is an on-line site of the now defunct magazine published by Yasser Seirawan. He still reports on some major events and editorialises there. He is also connected to **http://www.seattlechessfoundation.org**, which will run the US Championships in the near future.

Probably one of the more disappointing aspects on the Internet is the fractured coverage of American chess. However, there are some sites worth checking out for individual events. These include:

Michael Atkins site at **http://www.wizard.net/~matkins**.
The World Open in Philadelphia at **http://www.worldopen.com**.
The Mechanics Institute Tournament in San Francisco at **http://www.chessclub.org**.
The famous Marshall Chess Club at **http://www.marshallchessclub.org**.

The US Chess Federation (**http://www.uschess.org**) doesn't seem to collect games and results from its region, but it might be worth checking if there have been changes in this area.

Other sites of interest

Hellas Chess Club **http://www.chess.gr** (Greece)
Hellir Chess Club **http://simnet.is/hellir** (Iceland)
Brazilian Chess Federation **http://www.cbx.org.br**
British Chess Federation **http://www.bcf.ndirect.co.uk**
Dutch Chess Federation **http://www.schaakbond.nl**
Slovenian Chess Federation **http://www.sah-zveza.si**
Hungarian Chess Federation **http://www.chess.hu**
Chess News from Argentina especially **http://www.adrianroldan.com**
Ruschess site **http://www.ruschess.com**
Australian Chess Federation **http://www.auschess.org.au**
Sam Sloan's Chess Page **http://www.samsloan.com/chess.htm** or
http://www.ishipress.com/chess.htm
World Chess Council (Valery Salov's organisation) **http://ajedrez_democratico.tripod.com**

This is, however, really a random selection of chess sites worldwide and you should investigate the Federation and News sites I give in the links section for yourself.

Chess Newsgroups

The chess newsgroups are amongst the oldest fixtures on the Internet. A freewheeling and uncensored forum, they can be in turn be informative, irritating, unreliable, libellous, surprising, and most of all, compulsive. They are in effect emails that can be read by everybody. Someone posts some news or views and then anyone can reply to that. This then forms into something that is known as a thread following on from the same topic (although discussions can fly off at weird tangents). You will get to hear the most important news stories, sometimes quicker than anywhere else.

The main chess group is rec.games.chess.misc and there is a FAQ (Frequently Asked Questions) associated with it, written by Steve Pribut. This can be be read at **http://www.clark.net/pub/pribut/chess.html**. I think everyone who has used the newsgroups has at some time or other posted things they've later regretted. You can get terribly annoyed with what you read there and post very intemperate things in return. Take a deep breath if you're losing your temper and ask yourself if it's worth it. Of course, some people love a good argument and if you do it might be the place for you, although people will probably come to hate you for it!

The main newsgroups are:

rec.games.chess.misc (general topics)
rec.games.chess.politics (chess politics was formed to keep in particular discussion of the United States Chess Federation affairs away from the ears of the masses)
rec.games.chess.analysis (analysis of chess games)
rec.games.chess.play-by-mail (correspondence and email chess)

rec.games.chess.computer (computer chess).

These have the vast majority of traffic. There are other regional and specialist news-groups, some with almost no traffic but others that are quite active. Some of the most important ones are:

de.alt.games.schach
it.hobby.scacchi
alt.chess.ics
nl.sport.schaken
fr.rec.jeux.echecs

Discussion Boards

Bulletin board discussion groups are similar to the newsgroups, but capable of some censorship (you can be thrown off for bad language or very inflammatory postings, nut almost never for your point of view). Some come and go, but below are all the established bulletin boards. You'll need to sign up for them before being able to post.

About.com Chess Bulletin Board **http://forums.about.com/ab-chess/start**
Bulletin Board **http://f11.parsimony.net/forum16635**
Chess Café Bulletin Board **http://www.chesscafe.com/board/board.htm**
Computer Chess Club **http://www.icdchess.com**

PGN Format – The Easy Guide

The smallest amount you need to know about PGN is that it's a text file format for transmitting games. If you see a link to PGN games, say for a tournament or perhaps an opening, you can click on it and your browser should offer to save the file to disk. If your browser doesn't offer this you can force it to save to disk by right clicking on the link and using the option 'save target as'). Then you can open the file you've saved to disk in many chess programs and it should allow you to see a list of games within the file and play through them.

PGN being a text format means you can also open the file in a text editor or word processor and just read the contents. PGN is designed to work on many systems; it isn't designed for compactness. Sometimes PGN files are compressed or zipped (the file name will end in .zip). In this case you need an unzipping program such as Winzip (**http://www.winzip.com**) to unpack the files and end up with the original PGN file.

PGN Format –The Technical Guide

PGN (or portable game notation) is the format of choice for transmitting games on the Internet. The current standard was finished in 1994 and it enabled chess software writers to be able to write their programs to take it into account. Interested parties wrote the standard after consultation on the Internet, an effort co-ordinated by Steven J. Edwards. The format uses ASCII text files to transmit the data. This means that different computer systems (Windows, DOS, Mac, UNIX) can read the same file. There are two kinds of file you'll meet on the Internet: text files and binary files. Binary files such as zip files, or indeed things like word processing files (e.g. Microsoft Word files) can be infected by viruses; text files cannot. The whole standard should allow for interchange of data between different database systems (i.e. you should be able to convert a file in ChessBase into PGN and then that PGN to any other chess database system).

Here are two examples PGN games: the first game is given by the PGN standard itself. You should have no fewer tags than this example with the seven basic tags (everything between the inverted commas is the information unique to the game). The second game has some additional (supplemental) tags. A PGN file of such games would have a number of these games separated by at least a double carriage return.

[Event "F/S Return Match"]
[Site "Belgrade, Serbia JUG"]
[Date "1992.11.04"]
[Round "29"]
[White "Fischer, Robert J."]
[Black "Spassky, Boris V."]
[Result "1/2-1/2"]

1. e4 e5 2. Nf3 Nc6 3. Bb5 a6 4. Ba4 Nf6 5. O-O Be7 6. Re1 b5 7. Bb3 d6 8. c3 O-O 9. h3 Nb8 10. d4 Nbd7 11. c4 c6 12. cxb5 axb5 13. Nc3 Bb7 14. Bg5 b4 15. Nb1 h6 16. Bh4 c5 17. dxe5 Nxe4 18. Bxe7 Qxe7 19. exd6 Qf6 20. Nbd2 Nxd6 21. Nc4 Nxc4 22. Bxc4 Nb6 23. Ne5 Rae8 24. Bxf7+ Rxf7 25. Nxf7 Rxe1+ 26. Qxe1 Kxf7 27. Qe3 Qg5 28. Qxg5 hxg5 29. b3 Ke6 30. a3 Kd6 31. axb4 cxb4 32. Ra5 Nd5 33. f3 Bc8 34. Kf2 Bf5 35. Ra7 g6 36. Ra6+ Kc5 37. Ke1 Nf4 38. g3 Nxh3 39. Kd2 Kb5 40. Rd6 Kc5 41. Ra6 Nf2 42. g4 Bd3 43. Re6 1/2-1/2

[Event "Corus"]
[Site "Wijk aan Zee NED"]
[Date "2001.01.23"]
[Round "9"]
[White "Kasparov, Garry"]
[Black "Shirov, Alexei"]
[Result "1-0"]
[WhiteElo "2849"]
[BlackElo "2718"]
[EventDate "2001.01.13"]
[ECO "C42"]

1. e4 e5 2. Nf3 Nf6 3. Nxe5 d6 4. Nf3 Nxe4 5. d4 d5 6. Bd3 Bd6 7. O-O O-O 8. c4 c6 9. Qc2 Na6 10. a3 Bg4 11. Ne5 Bh5 12. cxd5 cxd5 13. Nc3 Nxc3 14. bxc3 Kh8 15. f4 Bxe5 16. fxe5 Bg6 17. a4 Qd7 18. Ba3 Rfe8 19. Bxg6 fxg6 20. Qb3 b6 21. Bd6 Nc7 22. Rf3 Rac8 23. Raf1 h6 24. Qc2 Qg4 25. Rg3 Qh5 26. Rh3 Qg5 27. Rg3 Qh5 28. Bxc7 Rxc7 29. Rxg6 Qh4 30. h3 Qxd4+ 31. cxd4 Rxc2 32. Rf7 Rg8 33. Rd6 Rc4 34. Rxd5 Rxa4 35. Rdd7 Ra1+ 36. Kf2 Ra2+ 37. Kf3 Kh7 38. e6 Kg6 39. d5 Rc8 40. Rc7 Re8 41. g4 a5 42. Rxg7+ Kf6 43. Rgf7+ Ke5 44. Rf5+ Kd4 45. e7 1-0

Most of the tags at the top of the game are reasonably self-explanatory. [Event ""],

[Site ""] and [Date ""] contain the information about when and where the event took place. The country should be signified by the three letter International Olympic Committee country codes (e.g. Germany GER, United States of America USA, Spain ESP etc.).

The round numbers are generally easy too. In the case of knockout events, [Round "3.1"], [Round "3.2"], and [Round "3.3"] etc. would signify the first three games played in round three of a knockout event. In the case of the tags for the players, [White "Fischer, Robert J."] [Black "Spassky, Boris V."] are of the form 'surname comma space first names'. The standard recommends using the FIDE rating list for the names; given the amount of ways to spell some names, this is excellent advice. TWIC uses a short form of the first names, which was especially useful with the old ChessBase format, which lacked space for very long names. I still use them to remain consistent.

There are only four possible results: win for Black [Result "0-1"], win for White [Result "1-0"], draw [Result "1/2-1/2"] and [Result "*"], which means game unfinished or result otherwise unknown (this should be used in PGN to cover live games for instance).

Of the additional tags, [EventDate "2001.01.13"] gives the start date of the event. This tag can be used to clarify events which start in one year and finish in another (for example, Hastings traditionally takes place over a new year – this can confuse some programs).

Once the main tags have been filled in there is the move text section. This should be in standard algebraic notation (SAN) but this is tougher than it first appears. You should always use a computer program to generate SAN, but even then SAN, as given in the PGN standard, is rare. Nevertheless most mainstream programs are good enough for this purpose. One example of difference that doesn't matter is that the standard gives 1. e4 e6 2. d4 d5 3. Nc3 Bb4 4. exd5 exd5 5. Ne2, rather than 1. e4 e6 2. d4 d5 3. Nc3 Bb4 4. exd5 exd5 5. Nge2, as given by ChessBase, for example (the point is that 5 Nce2 is illegal as it would be check). In general the moves should be in short, algebraic format and non-ambiguous. If either rook can go to a square then this needs to be shown, for example Rac1 not Rc1 (these are easily overlooked if you try and type games in freehand).

You can use these annotations: '!', '?', '!!', '!?', '?!', and '??' (but not e.p. for en passant). You can put written annotations into the text surrounded with curly brackets, e.g. 1. e4 e6 2. d4 d5 3. Nc3 Bb4 {Black chooses the Winawer Variation} 4. exd5 {White plays a sideline} exd5 5. Nge2 etc. If you use ChessBase you will find variations appearing between single round brackets (), the use of which is not well documented. Below is an example of something that isn't really PGN at all and we still see many examples of quite strange formats pretending to be PGN on the Internet.

[Event "?"]
[Site "Troll Masters, Gausd"]
[Date "1995.??.??"]
[Round "1"]
[White "Schmittdiel,E"]
[Black "Kinsman,A"]
[Result "0-1"]
[ECO "C01"]

1. e2-e4 e7-e6 2. d2-d4 d7-d5 3. Nb1-c3 Bf8-b4 4. e4xd5 e6xd5 5. Ng1-e2 c7-c6 6. Bc1-f4 Ng8-e7 7. a2-a3 Bb4-d6 8. Qd1-d2 Ne7-g6 9. Bf4xd6 Qd8xd6 10. h2-h4 Bc8-e6 11. h4-h5 Ng6-e7 12. h5-h6 g7-g6 13. Ne2-f4 Nb8-d7 14. O-O-O O-O-O 15. Rd1-e1 Rd8-e8 16. Nc3-a4 Kc8-b8 17. g2-g3 Rh8-f8 18. Bf1-g2 Ne7-c8 19. Qd2-c3 Be6-f5 20. Na4-c5 Qd6-f6 21. Nf4-d3 Nd7xc5 22. Nd3xc5 Qf6-d8 23. Qc3-b4 Nc8-d6 24. b2-b3 b7-b6 25. Re1-e5 a7-a5 26. Nc5-d7 Qd8xd7 27. Qb4xb6 Nd6-b7 28. Rh1-e1 Re8xe5 29. d4xe5 Rf8-c8 30. Qb6-d4 Qd7-e7 31. Kc1-b2 Qe7-c5 32. Qd4-d2 Qc5-b6 33. f2-f3 a5-a4 34. g3-g4 Bf5-e6 35. b3-b4 d5-d4 36. Kb2-a1 Rc8-d8 37. g4-g5 Qb6-b5 38. Qd2-c1 d4-d3 39. c2xd3 Qb5xd3 0-1

Import and export

The standard states for anyone writing a chess program should be that it is generous in allowing many forms of algebraic notation when importing games, but rigorous in sticking to the standard in exporting games. That is, the above game should be acceptable for importing but you should never allow your program to create anything like that.

In ChessBase there is a useful feature whereby you can create a blank PGN game, drop moves into the window and then 'resave' the game with the moves. The converter they use is extremely generous. For example, it allows moves recorded in German algebraic notation.

The PGN standard can be found on the Internet in a number of places (just search for 'PGN Standard') including the University of Pittsburgh ftp site **http://www.pitt.edu/~schach**. It describes many of the complex issues here plus others, such as being able to set up starting positions using FEN (Forsyth-Edwards Notation).

Chess Data On-line

All or most of the above sites carry chess games. There is an important area of law to be discussed here, as games are copied, stored and redistributed across the Internet. Although FIDE spoke of attempting to establish copyright of chess games (residing with the players and by contract the organisers) there has been nearly a century of understanding that this cannot be done, and all the legal opinion I've heard says this is the way things will remain. In addition, recently the question of whether live broadcasts can receive some protection has been discussed. This has never been settled legally, but I believe the balance of opinion is that it *is* possible to rebroadcast games that appear live on the Internet on another site without permission. There is a final question as to whether game collections can be protected (for instance, ChessBase's own database it sells with its products). It seems they do receive some protection, but that it is comparatively light. In these last two cases I'm not entirely sure and the final rules may have to be settled some day in a court of law. A final warning to anyone who wishes to distribute games on the Internet: make sure all the annotations are removed, they most definitely have a copyright. However, permissiveness is clearly good for the chess community at large. Many people are interested in collecting as many games as they can, or games by a specific player or opening. There are a growing number of such data sites worldwide, although there comes a time when buying a CD of games becomes effective against the cost of download time.

The quality of game collections on the Internet is quite low in general. People mix and match games from a great number of sources and also use various programs to cut out duplicates. This means many collections have duplicate versions of the same game, multiple spellings of players' names and players' names incorrectly combined together when they are in fact different players.

The grandfather of all Internet download sites is the University of Pittsburgh chess site at **http://www.pitt.edu/~schach**. It's a major place to download software, but also it has PGN and ChessBase format files of games of every imaginable sort; if you want a classic tournament it's almost certain to be there.

Another site, which has set itself up far more recently, is called ChessLab (**http://www.chesslab.com**). This advertises itself as having two million interactive games on-line. Where they came from is one of the unclear points (I'm not happy that TWIC seems to copied without permission but what to do?) but this isn't an issue for the user of the site. It's a place to do a quick check for all sorts of game searches you might like to carry out. Using their Java Interface, you can search by player, result and date, and save the results in PGN.

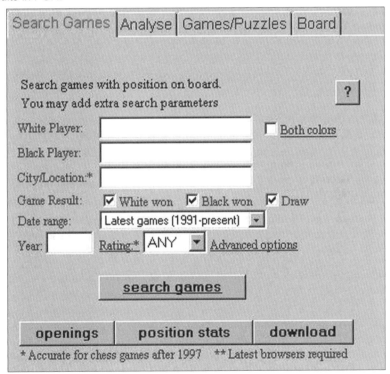

The search facility on chesslab.com

In a clear response to ChessLab, ChessBase set up its own service **http://www.chessbase-online.com**. This is a similar service, using ChessBase's own database, which they've maintained over the years. This database is reasonably accepted as being as accurate as they come. You can search using their new ChessBase 8 or via a Java client.

Although my focus has always been on news the TWIC weekly games section (**http://www.chesscenter.com/twic/twic.html**) contains a pretty consistent set of games that you can download and put together week by week. I have improved the headers of the games and they should slot together to make a database of reasonable quality. In terms of games by the leading players, there aren't many missing.

Review

Category: Chess Games
Site Name: University of Pittsburgh Chess Page
URL: **http://www.pitt.edu/~schach** (Alternative URL: **ftp://ftp.pitt.edu/group/chess**)
Country: US
Language: English

My comments

More specifically it's the Chess Archives page (**http://www.pitt.edu/~schach/Archives/index2.html**) that gives this site its popularity. I have no idea how long the site has been going, but from very early 1992 would be my guess. The site is basically an anonymous ftp site (hence the alternative address above) with a huge number of user compiled files. I believe Doug Attig has been the webmaster for many years.

The site has a very basic structure. On the left-hand side is the navigation to the different directories. The sections are:

Newstuff (you can check here for the latest additions to the library)

Games Collections in various file formats (Chess Assistant, ChessBase, PGN, NIC Base, Bookup)

Chess Materials (The Electronic Chess Library, Graphics and Art, Chess Playing Programs, Education, Organisations, Desktop Publishing, ASCII Text Files, Software Reviews, Chess News, Utilities)

Conversion Utilities – if you have chess files in a certain file format you may not need the program they were designed for in order to access them. An example is the ca2pgn3.zip file, which contains a converter for ChessAssistant files to pgn. There are some old friends there, such as the cbascii program (cba3216.zip), which is a converter for pgn to old ChessBase format and back again (one I still make use of in spite of having ChessBase myself). Also here are the nic2pgn and cb2pgn programs, which used to produce pgn that wasn't a form of pgn I recognise.

The site is most actively updated in the games section. Files from all recent events, as well as older events (the most recently added files when I visited were the 1962 British Championships, 1980 Hastings and 1984 Bugojno; the site is worth visiting if you need to study a classic tournament). I believe that the ChessBase, ChessAssistant and PGN sections generally cover the same events in different file formats. The NicBase directory doesn't seem to be updated as much, as it is a virtually defunct program now. The game sections (I'm taking the PGN directory as my example) are divided into the following:

Collections (an example of which is all World Championship games in the file wchamppg.zip)

Demo (this seems slightly misplaced but includes programs that can read pgn. An example is pgnread, which is a small program that allows you to display games)

Events (individual tournaments arranged by year)

Openings (a huge collection of files arranged by opening)

Players (a collection of games arranged by player).

If you access the program using Explorer you may get the message 'Running a system command on this item might be unsafe. Do you wish to continue?' Here I believe it is safe to continue, as it is a site that has a good record for system safety. You will need to have a compression program such as Winzip to unpack the files.

```
SITE: UNIV OF PITTSBURG CHESS PAGE
PRESENTATION        ✓ ✓ ✓ ✗ ✗
CONTENT             ✓ ✓ ✓ ✓ ✓
USER FRIENDLY       ✓ ✓ ✗ ✗ ✗
OVERALL             ✓ ✓ ✓ ✓ ✗
```

Review

Category: Chess Games
Site Name: Downloadable chess-games around the internet
URL: http://www.rhrk.uni-kl.de/~balzer/chessgames.html
Country: Germany
Language: English

My comments

Lars Balzer's links to downloadable chess games around the Internet.

Review

Category: Chess Games
Site Name: German site
URL: http://www.chess-international.de/
Country: Germany
Language: German

My comments

Hundreds and thousands of games downloadable from this site.

A Bit of History

From the late 1980s to 1992 news spread by disc through the post, with companies such as ChessBase and NicBase taking the lead. There were informal networks of journalists and players, while computer networks, such as the Compuserve Chess Forum, and other bulletin board systems were also a source of news. The electronic revolution of chess was starting.

In 1992 Bobby Fischer returned to play against Boris Spassky in a sanctions busting match in Yugoslavia. The games were covered semi-live on the Internet, the moves being spread by the use of a finger source, an extremely simple way of transmitting a small amount of data.

In 1993 there were almost daily updates of game files from the Linares tournament and towards the end of the year the PCA World Championship match between Kasparov and Short in London was transmitted from the venue, again using a finger source. The end of the year saw Anjo Anjewierden provide excellent coverage of the PCA qualifier in Groningen on the Internet.

1994 saw the real start of the World Wide Web, with internet pages and browsers. From this time on it was easy to set up a web site, and if you were at the venue, transmit the moves. Many events were not live but the moves and results started to become generally available. Dutch Teletext became available on the Internet. It brought live chess for major Dutch events for the first time. The year was scarred by reports from the FIDE Congress in Moscow of intimidation and threats. This was the first time delegates could report every day on the normally secret goings on within FIDE.

1995 saw the Kasparov-Anand PCA World Championship in New York. There was no official website but moves were readily available from the venue. Around this time TASC, who provided electronic boards for major events, also started broadcasting them on the Internet (**http://www.tasc.nl**); this quickly led to competitors having to do this too.

1996 started with the ACM Man Machine Challenge between Garry Kasparov and Deep Blue (the first match, which Kasparov won). IBM provided the website, got 5 million hits over the first weekend, and then had problems coping. Their coverage really marked a watershed; within a year almost every major event was covered by the organisers on the Internet. 1996 also saw events in Spain start to get Internet coverage. Net64 (now **http://www.ajedrez21.com**) covered events such as those in Madrid.

1997 was the year of the Deep Blue vs. Kasparov rematch, which gained unprecedented hits. This was a match that was both of interest to chess players, and perhaps even more, programmers. It really caught the public imagination.

White: DEEP BLUE
Black: Garry Kasparov
IBM Man vs. Machine, New York 1997
Ruy Lopez

1 e4 e5 2 ♘f3 ♘c6 3 ♗b5 a6 4 ♗a4 ♘f6 5 0-0 ♗e7 6 ♖e1 b5 7 ♗b3 d6 8 c3 0-0 9 h3 h6 10 d4 ♖e8 11 ♘bd2 ♗f8 12 ♘f1 ♗d7 13 ♘g3 ♘a5 14 ♗c2 c5 15 b3 ♘c6 16 d5 ♘e7 17 ♗e3 ♘g6 18 ♕d2 ♘h7 19 a4 ♘h4 20 ♘xh4 ♕xh4 21 ♕e2 ♕d8 22 b4 ♕c7 23 ♖ec1 c4 24 ♖a3 ♖ec8 25 ♖ca1 ♕d8

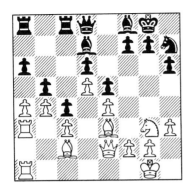

26 f4

'A stunning move played by a computer. Human beings know very well that opening a second front against a position under pressure can often cause it to collapse completely, but for a computer to find this idea is exceptional. None of the home computer programs I tested found this

move at a tournament time-limit.' – Nunn.

26...♘f6 27 fxe5 dxe5 28 ♕f1 ♘e8 29 ♕f2 ♘d6 30 ♗b6 ♕e8 31 ♖3a2 ♗e7 32 ♗c5 ♗f8 33 ♘f5 ♗xf5 34 exf5 f6 35 ♗xd6 ♗xd6 36 axb5 axb5 37 ♗e4 ♖xa2 38 ♕xa2 ♕d7 39 ♕a7 ♖c7 40 ♕b6 ♖b7 41 ♖a8+ ♔f7 42 ♕a6 ♕c7 43 ♕c6 ♕b6+ 44 ♔f1 ♖b8 45 ♖a6 1-0

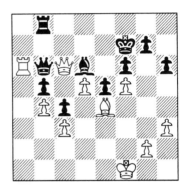

This game was followed by many chessplayers, not on the official IBM site, but on ICC. Kasparov resigned after 45 Ra6, but within a minute computer and GM analysis had established that Kasparov had missed a resource and had probably resigned in a drawn position; he should have continued with 45...Qe3!!.

The final game saw Kasparov allow a known piece sacrifice and blunder his way to a loss in only 19 moves, giving DEEP BLUE and IBM an undreamed of PR win. Much of this coverage is on the IBM site at **http://www.research.ibm.com/deepblue/home/html/b.html**.

In 1998 chess came of age on the Internet. We might be ready soon for another quantum leap, but essentially the all-embracing coverage of chess at the highest level we see now was in place. Since then two events, both involving Kasparov, stand out.

The first was the Kasparov vs. The World Challenge for the Microsoft Network. The match started in June 1999 and ran through until The World were finally beaten.

'The World' consisted of the public joining the MSN site to vote on suggestions by a team of top junior players including Etienne Bacrot, 16, Florin Felecan, 19, Irina Krush, 15, and Elisabeth Pähtz, 14. In particular the American star Irina Krush put a lot of effort into the game, but unfortunately there were voting irregularities (some thing which plagued a subsequent match). This meant that her suggestion of 51...Ka1, which should have drawn, was ignored. However, the game was a tremendous success for public participation and has been repeated a few times since on a smaller scale.

(**http://boards.gamers.com/messages/overview.asp?name=WTChess&page=1** is a good place to go and see if there are any current challenges and read about past problems.

Chess on the Net

White: Garry Kasparov
Black: The World
Internet MSN 1999
Sicilian Defence

1 e4 c5 2 ♘f3 d6 3 ♗b5+ ♗d7 4 ♗xd7+
♕xd7 5 c4 ♘c6 6 ♘c3 ♘f6 7 0-0 g6 8 d4
cxd4 9 ♘xd4 ♗g7 10 ♘de2 ♕e6 11 ♘d5
♕xe4 12 ♘c7+ ♔d7 13 ♘xa8 ♕xc4 14
♘b6+ axb6 15 ♘c3 ♖a8 16 a4 ♘e4 17
♘xe4 ♕xe4 18 ♕b3 f5 19 ♗g5 ♕b4 20
♕f7 ♗e5 21 h3 ♖xa4 22 ♖xa4 ♕xa4 23
♕xh7 ♗xb2 24 ♕xg6 ♕e4 25 ♕f7 ♗d4 26
♕b3 f4 27 ♕f7 ♗e5 28 h4 b5 29 h5 ♕c4
30 ♕f5+ ♕e6 31 ♕xe6+ ♔xe6 32 g3 fxg3
33 fxg3 b4 34 ♗f4 ♗d4+ 35 ♔h1 b3 36
g4 ♔d5 37 g5 e6 38 h6 ♘e7 39 ♖d1 e5 40
♗e3 ♔c4 41 ♗xd4 exd4 42 ♔g2 b2 43
♔f3 ♔c3 44 h7 ♘g6 45 ♔e4 ♔c2 46 ♖h1

d3 47 ♔f5 b1♕ 48 ♖xb1 ♔xb1 49 ♔xg6
d2 50 h8♕ d1♕ 51 ♕h7

51...b5 52 ♔f6+ ♔b2 53 ♕h2+ ♔a1 54
♕f4 b4 55 ♕xb4 ♕f3+ 56 ♔g7 d5 57
♕d4+ ♔b1 58 g6 ♕e4 59 ♕g1+ ♔b2 60
♕f2+ ♔c1 61 ♔f6 d4 62 g7 1-0

Much more can be found out about this game on the official website
http://www.zone.com/kasparov.

The second event was Kasparov's loss to Kramnik in the Brain Games World Championship in 2000. The event was not only covered live by the official site
http://www.braingames.net, but also the London Chess Centre
http://www.chesscenter.com/wcc2000, Kasparov.com and ICC. Legal advice around the time suggests that live coverage by the official site can't be protected and retransmission of moves from that site is possible without permission. There was also a first with
http://www.canalweb.com having a live video feed throughout the match, with commentary and pictures from the hall. This is something that looks like it should become standard.

Chapter Five

Commercial Chess Sites

Much of the material on the Internet is free. As you will have seen in other chapters, the amount of chess material out there is simply enormous. In the early 1990s, with academic institutions dominating, there was a real feeling at the time that the arrival of commerce would be a bad thing. Many of the standards and ideas that underpin the way chess is covered on the Internet came from the idea that by working together it would be possible to have everything for free by a huge community effort. The first wave of enthusiasm for E-commerce came in the mid-1990s and with the arrival of business there was a separate competing ethos. It would surely be possible to make a fortune on the Internet with so many new potential customers out there. Share prices have fallen, risen and fallen again since then, but there is no doubt that now much of our buying is already being done on the Internet. In chess almost all sites carry some sort of commercial connection. The more successful a site is, the more the overheads are.

Charging for a chess service provided on the Internet is still very rare. There are established examples in ICC (**http://www.chessclub.com**) and in the openings survey Chess Publishing (**http://www.chesspublishing.com**), and new and unproven ones in the Kasparovchess.com University and Chess Today (**http://www.chesstoday.net**). Part of the problem for commercial ventures is that the culture of the Internet is still very much 'everything for free'. This culture may be about to change, with some very big commercial concerns looking into selling films and music over the Internet. At several points in the time I've been on the Internet and thought about the concept of micro-payments for services rendered. I was reminded of it recently in an article on the highly interesting site Alertbox (**http://www.useit.com/alertbox**), where the net author Dr. Jakob Nielsen talks about current net issues. His 24th December 2000 article
(**http://www.useit.com/alertbox/20001224.html**) predicted in summary that '...offering free services on websites is not a sustainable business model, nor is advertising, which doesn't work on the web. Most Internet companies are now pursuing an enterprise strategy to make money, but they'll soon begin turning to individual customers for revenue as well.'

The Micro-payment concept goes like this: people aren't prepared to pay out $5 for a lot

of services provided but they might be persuaded to pay out 25 cents for a small service, like a download, if it was quick an easy to make those payments. In addition credit card transactions have an overhead for the seller so they can't ask for small payments even if they wanted to (graphically explained in a nice cartoon at:
http://www.thecomicreader.com/html/icst/icst-5/icst-5.html). I don't believe there will be a huge advance in the way chess is covered on the Internet without some sort of culture of payment, although what we have is very good. I've been through the period when this was a very popular concept around 1997, and by the following year no one was talking about it. It remains to be seen if Nielsen's prediction comes true in the next couple of years.

At the moment in chess, although advertising does provide some revenue, the largest single contributor to meeting the expense of most chess websites is commerce or a bene-factor. My experience in shopping on the Internet for chess goods is not very extensive; when you receive a lot of complimentary books and software the need doesn't tend to arise. I do, however, do quite a bit of shopping for books and CDs there. For myself it's not the price (although shopping on the Internet is very competitive), it's the sheer range. Many of the items I've bought on the Internet I simply would never have known about oth-erwise, never mind bought.

Even though you don't need a credit card to shop on the Internet, it is much easier to do it with one. This brings with it security considerations. I wouldn't want to dismiss worries about shopping on the Internet using a credit card, but they can be over exaggerated. Using a credit card over the Internet is pretty safe, provided you exercise some reason-able care. It certainly isn't anymore risky than giving the details over the phone or in some foreign countries on holiday. It should also be the case that your purchase is covered by some protection from your credit card company. That said, if you do feel uncomfortable about it there are a number of sensible precautions you can make.

Firstly take a good look at the site you're shopping from.

Are your personal details being sent to a secure server?

Both the Microsoft Internet Explorer and Netscape browsers are set up to allow encrypted transfer of information over the Internet. You can tell if you're entering a secure server because firstly, you may get a warning (unless you turned this option off yourself) and secondly, a padlock will appear on the left-hand side of the tiny globe in the bottom right hand corner of the page. Never send your credit card details by email; this method of communication is insecure.

The following give an indication of what you should look for before shopping at a particu-lar on-line site.

- Does it show signs of being updated recently?
- Does it look hastily and cheaply put together?
- Does it offer a number of ways of getting in touch with the company?
- Do you have any reason to suspect it is in financial trouble?
- Or is there just something about the site that's bothering you but you can't put your finger on it?

You might decide that you're not happy about something. You have a number of choices. One is to go to a newsgroup like rec.games.chess.misc and ask if anyone has shopped there (or even before posting the message, search the archives at a place like **http://www.dejanews.com** – now at the moment of writing changing to **http://groups.google.com**) to see if there are references.

Secondly, you could try emailing a query to the company. Find out if you get a quick reply or indeed any reply at all. In general if there is only an email contact and not a real world address and telephone number this should at least put you on your guard.

Thirdly, you could try calling them. If you're not happy about sending your details over the Internet but are happy using the phone to do this by all means do so, although sometimes this could be expensive if it's an international call (some companies have toll free calls).

Fourthly, you could in fact send a cheque or an international money order, instead of using a credit card. As I said before, a lot of the attraction is having the opportunity to purchase items you wouldn't ordinarily get the opportunity to.

Finally, and I think this applies to most stores on the Internet, buy something of low cost at first. Find out how you are treated as a customer. Is your credit card charged promptly? (major stores do this, but some save up the orders for some time to process them all at once – this can leave temptation in the way of a dishonest staff member). Are the goods dispatched promptly and do they arrive in good condition? The best stores work hard in gaining the trust and loyalty of their customers.

One study revealed that it took an average of a year to get used to the Internet enough to make an on-line purchase. I took five years! As in real life, use your common sense. If little warning bells are ringing telling you something might be wrong, don't go ahead with it – there are plenty of chess sites to buy from.

I have bought from individuals via E-Bay (**http://www.ebay.com**, although there are regional ones in the UK – **http://www.ebay.co.uk** – and individual ones in Austria, Australia, Canada, France, Germany, Italy and Japan as well). This is an on-line auction site as such you have to sort out payment between you. There are profiles of the people buying and selling on there (if they're not first time users) and this can tell you a little about the person. I bought a CD and paid for it by sending cash through the post after exchanging a couple of emails with the sender. This is convenient but not terribly secure, but buying in this kind of auction often leaves you having to find an alternative to a credit card, especially if the other person lives in another country, such as the US in this case. I hadn't even the slightest doubt the person was honest (although whether the money got there is always subject to prayer and the willingness in the end to accept a deal if it goes wrong). This isn't always the case, however.

Do remember, certainly in the case of the United Kingdom where you buy outside of the European Union such as in the States, that you may be liable for VAT and customs and excise duty, except for the smallest purchases (less than £18) or on books (where duty doesn't apply).

Probably the largest and most well known electronic retailer on the Internet is Amazon.com. They have a number of websites worldwide. The main American one

Chess on the Net

(**http://www.amazon.com**) is shadowed by regional ones in Germany, France, Japan and Britain (**http://www.amazon.co.uk**). They are pretty much the state of the art as far as purchasing is concerned and may be a good starting point for shopping on-line. Their chess section, however, is generally confined to the major chess publishers. You find things by searching their catalogue (there is no specialist section promoting new books on chess as there are with the major categories – you would have to search by author's name or title, or take pot luck with the word chess). I like amazon.com but wouldn't necessarily use it for chess.

Most chess stores sell the full range of goods. Chess books, software, sets, clocks are all sold on the Internet. It does mean that it has never been easier to buy just exactly what you want. I would add, however, that this is if you know what you want. In the case of books, you may have read a review or a passage from the book somewhere, or had it recommended, but you can't pick it up and look at it. This is true also of sets and clocks. I bought a pendant on the Internet once. It was exactly as the picture showed but it was tiny (I was fooled by their saying it was the large one; how small the small pendant was I really can't guess). So be careful and enquire if necessary for further details about what you're buying. If you buy a clock or a set which is cheap don't expect it to be of the highest quality (although you may be surprised). You get what you pay for (or maybe less than you pay for!) in this life and that isn't going to be altered on the Internet. A saving of a few pounds or dollars is perfectly possible on the Internet (but remember postage and packing will have to be included) but huge savings should ironically send the alarm bells ringing. In general you want good quality pictures of the goods, or a way of contacting the shop and checking exactly what you are buying. In the case of software, you may want to buy from a particular store but often you can go to the website of the software and download a demo version. These partially functional programs will give you a very good idea what you are going to get for your money and are one of the real plus points of the Internet; they can save you from really bad mistakes.

I'm not in a position to recommend one chess store above another, having really not used them in anger. I haven't heard of problems with any of the major chess retailers on the Internet but that doesn't mean there aren't any. Some sites are simply points of presence on the Internet for companies you might see at your local congress; others will have more sophisticated sites as their Internet sales are much larger. Every major commercial site discussed in this book has a chess store.

My TWIC site is hosted by the London Chess Centre (**http://www.chesscenter.com**), a shop in London which is also one of the major chess sites on the Internet, selling worldwide but specialising in US and British sales in particular. They sponsor TWIC and my job is to bring traffic; this is a typical situation in that popular websites need backing and chess shops need traffic. I list 31 sites in the index under shop but that list doesn't even include the sites more famous for their content.

Sites such as Kasparovchess.com (**http://www.kasparovchess.com**), Chess Café (**http://www.chesscafe.com**), Inside Chess (**http://www.insidechess.com**), British Chess Magazine **http://www.bcmchess.co.uk** and FIDE (**http://www.fide.com**) are amongst the more famous sites with chess shops. In addition, a number of chess suppliers have moved on to the Internet in a concerted way. Every country has a chess supplier and a full list would be very long. Some of the other major suppliers include: Chess 4 Less (**http://www.chess4less.com**), Chessco chess shop (**http://www.chessco.com**) and Your move chess and games (**http://chessusa.com**). A final site that doesn't quite slot in anywhere perfectly is the Smartchess Online site (World Wide Web Chess Superstore – **http://www.smartchess.com**), which is a mixture of publisher and shop, but also with material on some of the major chess events written by Ron Henley and full coverage of the career of Irina Krush. The also have connections to Shirov and Karpov but at the time of writing I couldn't easily find material on them.

Publishers

Chess book publishers themselves have started to get a presence on-line. The major chess publisher of books for many years was Batsford Chess Books (**http://www.batsford.com/Chess**). Then Batsford as a whole ran into financial trouble and Chrysalis books bought the chess catalogue. Their website covers new books as well as their back catalogue, along with an offer to join their book club.

Gambit Chess Publishers (**http://www.gambitchess.co.uk**) was formed by Grandmasters John Nunn and Murray Chandler, and FIDE Master Graham Burgess, after a number of years writing and editing for Batsford. Their website promotes the latest books from their catalogue and on-line sale via the British Chess Magazine.

This book is published by Everyman Chess, whose website is at **http://www.everyman.uk.com**. This follows a very similar approach to the above. The American publisher Avery Cardoza has a website for his chess publications called Chess City (**http://www.chesscity.com**). It advertises his books and also has a lot of extra material by Eric Schiller, including novice tips and other features. Schiller has his own website at **http://www.chessworks.com** but is in the process of transferring most of the chess material to the Chess City site, including his take on how new web protocols such as XML might be used in chess.

Other interesting publishers with material on the web include Pickard & Son (**http://www.chesscentral.com**), whose books are not only in conventional print – they've also branched out into electronic editions for some works, McFarland & Company (**http://www.mcfarlandpub.com**) and Schachverlag Kania (**http://www.kaniaverlag.de**).

Chess Magazines and Publications

Chess magazines also have challenges to meet with the advent of the Internet. In the past, the first chess fans might hear about major tournaments would be in the monthly chess magazines they subscribe to. Sometimes the postings were so out of date that they could be up to two months after the actual event. Now, with every major event's games available on the Internet, they've had to improve the features and insight into the game; it's simply insufficient to give raw game scores anymore. Almost every major country has a magazine and most not only cover international events of major importance, but also their own local chess scene.

A large number of these magazines also have their own websites. Often these sites are a good place to find regional chess news and calendars of upcoming regional events. Printed magazines with additional useful content on the Internet also are numerous. Here's a brief survey of key sites:

New in Chess http://www.newinchess.com

This includes free downloads of games to go with its magazine, a vast links section and a shop for all its products. This is one of the most famous chess publications for the serious chess player has an interesting website.

Chess Informant http://www.sahovski.com

This has been the key publication for chess theory. They've embraced the modern age and have a free chess reader you can download from their site and a few free files to go with it (and it looks pretty good). They sell not only the hard copy but also electronic versions of their magazine. It's also the home for the Encyclopaedia of Chess Openings.

Europe-Echecs http://www.europe-echecs.com

Europe-Echecs is France's leading magazine on chess. Their website covers international chess news and also provide good and original coverage of French events. The whole site is in French.

Kingpin http://www.chesscenter.com/kingpin/Kingpin

One of the best-kept secrets of the British chess scene is *Kingpin*. The satirical chess magazine has been a regular recipient of the custom of the chess player who loses quickly on the morning of a congress and has a few hours to fill. The acid humour and sometimes *Private Eye* like revelations have appeared irregularly for at least a decade. There is an on-line section of articles now available. So if you want to know 'how to write a chess book and make loads of dosh' or read some of their famously disrespectful book reviews, this is the place to go. Oh, and you can order the magazine too.

British Chess Magazine http://www.bcmchess.co.uk

British Chess Magazine (founded 1881) not only publicises its magazine and shop but also has excellent coverage of the British chess scene on-line, along with a tournament calendar.

Chess http://www.chesscenter.com

British Chess Magazine's rival in the UK is *Chess*, which I guess has me as an attraction?!

Chess Life http://www.uschess.org/about/clife.html

This USCF production is the leading American magazine, although the website offers little more than a promotion of it.

Further a field Chess Mate, the *Indian Chess Magazine* has a website at **http://www.chess-mate.com**, which is good on the growing Indian chess scene. Ceskoslovensky Sach (**http://www.sach.cz**) is good for Czech news. In German there's *Schach* at **http://www.zeitschriftschach.de**, which has some news and a tournament calendar. It's rival *Schach Magazin 64* (**http://www.schach-magazin.de**) carries some interesting features from the magazine, including training and combinations.

There are many more across the world, if your language skills are up to it. A recent addition from an area of the World which is growing in strength by the year is Chess in China (**http://home.chinese.com/~chessinchina**); it is in Chinese, however.

Software

Commercial producers of software would be very foolish indeed if they didn't have an on-line site. Nowhere in the commercial arena on the Internet can a seller add more value to his or her product than here. In trading in goods such as books or chess sets, going to a normal shop allows you to try out the goods. It is quite rare that you can try out software (although in some shops it is possible). On the other hand, on the Internet a software company can produce demos for downloading. You can try the program out, get a feel for how it works and decide whether it is worth the money. You shouldn't be totally indis-criminate about downloading software; having lots of buggy, badly written programs on your computer can effect its performance, and downloading software from sites which don't explain who is responsible for them can leave you open to downloading a program that has malicious intent. Commercial software companies have a stake in making their demo versions as good as possible, they want you to buy from them and you in turn can save yourself from expensive mistakes.

Another reason why software companies need websites is that they can offer customer support. If you buy a program that doesn't have this on-line support and it doesn't work properly you're left with few easy options. Many programs have minor programming faults that need correcting. Both these needs can be met on the Internet. Updates and free ad-ditions to programs can be downloaded from the major software manufacturers sites and they should also be able to answer queries you have about the program. Staying in touch with the users of their programs can only be beneficial for the software company.

Although larger products may need to be put on a CD and sent to you, almost all software manufacturers will also sell smaller items to you via a download from the Internet, paid for by credit card.

Major chess software companies on-line include ChessBase (**http://www.chessbase.com**). With its ChessBase Database system, its many commercial playing programs (including Fritz and Junior) and its data and training packages, this company is the leading provider of software to the professional and keen amateur. Their website offers a large database of games, which can be searched on-line either with or without their program. They provide updates to their products, demos and announcements on their products. In terms of pro-fessional database products, ChessAssistant (**http://www.chessassistant.com**) is the only one that offers any real competition. They also sell data and training packages.

Chess playing programs with their own websites include Ed Shroeder's Rebel site (**http://www.rebel.nl**) and the biggest selling chess program of them all (**http://www.chessmaster.com**). Chessmaster has a website that allows on-line play using their program.

Chess training software is available from ChessBase and ChessAssistant but there are also specialists in this area. Chess Mentor (**http://www.chess.com**) produces software and books, teaching chess from absolute beginners up to reasonably advanced levels. Another such company is Chess Academy at **http://www.chessacademy.de**.

A new company on the Internet is Electronic Chess Books (**http://www.echessbook.com**), their first book being the Zurich 1953 tournament. In contrast Bookup (**http://www.bookup.com**) is one of the oldest established software companies on the Internet. They offer what they call a positional database system, which certainly works on a different principle to ChessBase and ChessAssistant. Another company that have been around quite a while is TASC (**http://www.tasc.nl**), with a number of commercial programs including a database system.

Its rare for one website to be so dominant but if you wish to read reviews about software products (and incidentally find out what is available in the first place) then certainly you should try Bob Pawlak's Chess Reviews (Free reviews of Chess Software and Products) site at **http://www.chessreviews.com**. I really can't recommend this site enough. Almost every significant product going back a number of years is here and the reviews seem to be objective enough (although if you rely on receiving products to review, perhaps going nuclear against a major manufacturer might be difficult). The reviews carry the kind of detail that allows you to really get a feeling for what you get for your money.

Chess Book Reviews

There are many specialist chess books released each year. It's always useful to have more information if you intend to buy them, but also a good review can whet the appetite, tell you everything you need to know about the book so you don't need to buy it or warn you off bad purchases.

John Elburg's Chessbookreviews Homepage at **http://www.chessmail.com/books** (hosted by the correspondence magazine Chessmail) is probably the most comprehensive set of book reviews on the Internet. The amount of material he gets through is simply enormous, not only books but also electronic chess products. There are criticisms of his reviews; English is not John Elburg's first language and most of his reviews tend to be favourable, even of books that others have considered truly awful. Nevertheless, there is a wealth of detail here about the books and what you get for your money, as well as information about how to get hold of the rarer publications. Definitely a good place to find out what's new, but possibly not to decide your purchase.

Possibly you might consider me biased, but John Watson's Book Reviews, which he sends to me and appear irregularly on the TWIC website at **http://www.chesscenter.com/twic/watson.html**, are acknowledged amongst the best on the Internet. John takes his time over the reviews and doesn't pull his punches when required. It would be wrong to say most of his reviews are negative, as he tends to study in detail those books that are inherently worthwhile. He reads the books he does review in detail, for instance looking at lines he knows in openings books, and thus can come to a balanced judgement. John has recently had to cut down the number of reviews he does but I expect at least a few will appear in the next year.

Another major on-line reviewer is Chess Café Book Reviews by Taylor Kingston and others at **http://www.chesscafe.com/REVIEWS/books.HTM**. There are regular reviews at the

Chess Café site and they are a good read in themselves. At the time of writing the site has a review of a book called *Super Nezh: Chess Assassin*, reviewed by Stephen Ham. This actually tells you a lot of the more interesting stories about the life of well respected Soviet player Rashid Nezhmetdinov, as well as giving one of the games from the book. There were 212 books reviewed in the archives at the time of writing, nothing like a complete set of reviews over this period of time but definitely worth consulting or indeed reading just on their own.

The chess section of the Mind Sports Olympiad site (**http://www.msoworld.com**) also has room for reviews. Stephen Leary writes them and he produces well-balanced and useful reviews. Another site with a good set of reviews and links is Randy's Revealing Reviews (**http://ourworld.compuserve.com/homepages/randybauer**); they also appear prominently on the Chessopolis site (**http://www.chessopolis.com**)

Other Review Sites worth looking at are:

Jeremy Silman's Book reviews for Inside Chess
(**http://www.insidechess.com./silman.html**)
Allan Savage's reviews for Chess Mail (**http://www.chessmail.com/savage_review.html**)
Tim Harding's review for Chess Mail (**http://www.chessmail.com/reviews.html**)
Chess Program Reviews (**http://www.chessreviews.com**)

Chapter Six

General Chess Interest

There are sites that don't really fall into a single category. I've called these sites general interest sites. What I have in mind here are sites with an accent on writing and entertainment.

One of the first stops anyone should make when first using the Internet for chess is Hannon Russell's Chess Café site (**http://www.chesscafe.com**). Hannon Russell is a chess writer and collector. Having started in 1996, Russell's site is one of the oldest sites on the Internet. As a mix of chess history, reviews and general chess writing it cannot be beaten. The material is well presented and there is always something of interest. The site is a business which sells chess books and sets, as well as a venture into electronic chess publishing with *Secret Matches: The Unpublished Training games of Mikhail Botvinnik*. Chess Café is neither overbearing nor a site that exceeds its reach. At the time of writing there are around twelve regular columnists who write exclusive articles for the site, as well as weekly book reviews, a very worth while discussion board and a new series of historic chess photos from the collection of the famous historian Edward Winter. Regular columns include: Endgame Corner by Karsten Müller, The Kibitzer by Tim Harding, The Instructor by Mark Dvoretsky, The Wanderer by Mike Franett, Checkpoint by Carsten Hansen, Opening Lanes by Gary Lane, Dutch Treat by Hans Ree, The Miles Report by Tony Miles, The Q & A Way by Bruce Pandolfini, Late Knight by Richard Forster and An Arbiter's Notebook by Geurt Gijssen. It is one of the most successful chess sites on the Internet and deservedly so.

Another site in a similar vein is Tim Krabbé's chess site at **http://www.xs4all.nl/~timkr/chess/chess.html**. Krabbé is a multitalented writer (author of a book which was made into the film *The Vanishing*) and journalist, as well as being a strong chess player who has his own web page. This site shows what can be achieved over a period of time of conscientious accumulative writing. He spreads his net wide, taking in chess trivia, problems, news and history and his site is regularly updated. His open chess diary ranges over an eclectic mix of topics. In recent times entries include mentions of chess in commentaries to other sports, a grotesque chess study, a continued watch for the dark right hand corner square mafia (photographs with the board the wrong way round) and the fate of Salo Landau during the second world war; this range is typical of the mix. He also has a chess records page which has become his speciality.

These are the categories:

Moves Category: Longest game, Shortest game, Longest series of moves by one piece, Longest symmetrical game, Latest castling, Greatest number of castlings,

Captures category: Latest first capture, Longest decisive game without a capture, Quickest exchange game, Longest consecutive series of captures, Longest sequence without captures, Longest en prise.

Checks category: Longest series of checks, Longest mutual series of checks, Greatest number of checks.

Promotion category: Greatest number of Queens, Longest 4-Queen sequence, Longest polygamy, Greatest number of Rooks, Greatest number of Knights, Longest 3-Knight sequence.

Pieces category: Longest immobility

Position category: Most passed pawns, Longest living quadrupled pawns, Earliest stalemate.

Add to this articles such as 'Games Page Historical – great and unusual games for online viewing & downloading', 'The 110 Greatest Moves ever played', 'Promotion to Rook and Bishop in Games – Over 40 serious examples', 'The Ultimate Blunder – Resigning in winning positions', 'Strangest coincidence ever – or hoax? The case of the Polish Rxb2', 'Alekhine's five Queen game', 'The Full Morphy: All his 415 known games for online viewing & downloading', 'The discovery of the Saavedra - the original 1895 Weekly Citizen columns' and you see it's a place worth going to.

Another site to take in and bookmark is the La Mecca Chess Encyclopaedia at **http://maskeret.com/mecca/index.shtml**. This site, produced by Italian Maurizio Mascheroni, is part links guide, part news site and part chess calendar, but what really separates it from the run of the mill site is the searchable chess encyclopaedia. It's a very good place to start if you're looking for a specific piece of information, especially if it's historical. The definitions are from all sorts of sources so the quality varies, but as a single starting point it's very good. Often links are included to other destinations on the Internet. Amongst the contributors is Bill Wall and you can check out his personal site at **http://www.geocities.com/SiliconValley/Lab/7378/chess.htm**.

Another destination mixing links and stories is **http://www.chessopolis.com**; this includes book reviews by Randy Bauer, Coffee Break Chess by Alexander Baburin (of which more in a moment), downloads and news.

The Mind Sports Olympiad has their own site at **http://www.msoworld.com**. This has a large range of topics covered on many games and brain issues and includes a sizable section on chess.

Player Sites

The above sites show just what can be achieved with knowledge, persistence and passion. The next big growth area I believe will be that of personal player sites. Players will only set up and write such sites if it is the their commercial advantage. I believe the time is coming where at least a minimal site for their own promotion will make sense. I'm not talking about a commercial venture such as **http://www.kasparovchess.com** here (although Kasparov uses it for his own annotations and interviews which gets his point of view across ahead of his rivals). However, it is sites such as **http://chess-sector.odessa.ua**, which has a section on the career of rising Ukrainian star Ruslan Ponomariov (with his co-operation at **http://chess-sector.odessa.ua/ruslan.html**) that I would like to see more of. This site includes all the key dates in his career, games, annotations, links to other materials as well as contact information.

Susan Polgar has a more commercially oriented site at **http://www.polgarchess.com** which mostly promotes her books and exhibitions (although it also gives her point of view about her dispute with FIDE and family information). At the time of writing the site needed updating. Her sister Judit doesn't have her own website and nature abhors a vacuum: **http://www.controltheweb.com/polgar** has lots of pictures of her as well as giving career details. There is definite justification for Judit Polgar herself to have a website. A similar problem is to been seen with Viswanathan Anand in that he doesn't have his own web pages, so someone has produced a fan page at **http://www.geocities.com/Colosseum/Slope/4448**, which is probably closer to the kind of image Anand might wish to present than the Polgar pages. Of course you could get a person writing a really mischievous site about you. The Klub Karpov site (World Champion: Before, Now, Forever!) at **http://www.geocities.com/WallStreet/District/9917/klubkarpov.html** doesn't pretend to be anything other than a chess satire, but it does raise a smile.

Of course, there are famous players who for whatever reason are unlikely to produce websites of their own. Bobby Fischer has a number of sites devoted to him, examples of which are the Bobby Fischer Links page at **http://www.chesslinks.org/hof/fischer.html**, The Bobby Fischer Homepage at **http://www.rio.com/~johnnymc** and The Bobby Fischer Page at **http://queen.chessclub.com/philchess/bobby.htm**. This final site has recordings of interviews Fischer gave in 1999 and 2000 on Philippino radio (a warning – these interviews contain strong language and express strong anti-Semitic views). He, of course, could produce his own web page if he chose, although whether people think that would be a good thing is another question.

Many famous players have game collections on the Internet. A great place to start would be University of Pittsburgh Chess archive at **http://www.pitt.edu/~schach**. If you search hard enough there are pages on players such as David Bronstein (**http://davidbronstein.metropoli2000.net**) and Mikhail Tal (**http://www.jthin.co.uk/tal.htm**). Also worth checking out is **http://www.mark-weeks.com/chess/wcc-indx.htm**, which is Mark Week's World Chess Championship site.

Another two sites worth looking at are Chess Archaeology at **http://www.chessarch.com**, which has photos and research (although it doesn't seem to be that active at the moment) and **http://www.chesshistory.com**, which might become important in the future as it outlines projects that people may like to work on.

Slowly there is the recognition amongst active chess players that a personal site is good for their own business. Gregory Kaidanov is now a professional player in the US who also teaches. For some time he had a private publication called the *Kaidanov Report* and he also has a web presence at **http://members.iglou.com/kaidanov**.

A very readable but trenchant view of the chess world is to be found on Alex Yermolinsky's own webpages at **http://www.concentric.net/~Yermo**. Another recent entry into the ranks are Sergei Tiviakov's webpages at **http://www.tiviakov.demon.nl/index.htm**, which are English and Russian, although he has recently started living in The Netherlands and is considered a Dutch player now. He annotates some games and talks about his career. Jaan Ehlvest's homesite at **http://www.ehlvest.com** also follows a similar approach.

Perhaps the player who in recent times has embraced the web most is Alex Baburin. For some time now he has produced a regular newsletter on his own career called Coffee Break (30 by January 2001), which includes news, views, adverts for his own enterprises and more. He recently branched out, producing two more websites. One site he describes as the first a daily chess magazine *Chess Today* (**http://www.chesstoday.net**). This costs around $15 for four months. The second site is gmsquare (**http://www.gmsquare.com**). This site is the home for his website, as well as those of Lev Psakhis and most interestingly, Alexander Morozevich. In what is a pretty obvious idea in retrospect, they hope to provide web presences for Grandmasters with limited knowledge or time to do it themselves. This could be one to watch.

Newspaper Chess Columns

Another area to find general interest material is the newspaper chess column. Not all the best columns by any means are published by their newspapers in their on-line editions, but there are a few worth looking at. In the news section of the book I mentioned **http://www.elpais.es** with Leontxo Garcia and **http://www.the-hindu.com** with Arvind Aaron as good sources for news. There are some slightly less timely columns that are worth a read however. Lubosh Kavalek's *Washington Post* column is published on the newspapers website **http://www.washingtonpost.com/wp-dyn/style/columns/chess**, as is the column by Robert Byrne in the *New York Times* at **http://www.nytimes.com/diversions/chess**. In England there are many good chess columnists. However, the only one available on the Internet is Ray Keene's in *The Times* at **http://www.thetimes.co.uk**. I can only see this roster increasing over the next few years so it's worth searching the websites of newspapers with columnists you like just to see if they get added. A newspaper which has a chess columnist is also generally favourable to chess; they do cover the major chess news stories in their main sections.

Champion loses

Today's game sees world champion Kramnik losing to a dangerous rival in the blindfold section of the Amber tournament in Monaco.

White: Veselin Topalov
Black: Vladimir Kramnik
Monaco Blindfold 2001
Queen's Gambit Declined

1 d4 Nf6 2 c4 e6 3 Nf3 d5 4 Nc3 Be7 5 Bf4 0-0 6 e3 c5 7 dxc5 Bxc5 8 a3

The Bf4 line of the Queen's Gambit is also a favourite of Kramnik who used it against Nigel Short in the Wijk aan Zee tournament in 2000. That game went 8 cxd5 Nxd5 9 Nxd5 exd5 10 a3 Nc6 11 Bd3 and Kramnik went on to win.

8 ... Nc6 9 Qc2 Qa5 10 Nd2

Another dangerous line for Black here is 10 0-0-0 as seen in Speelman - Short, Candidates Match, London 1988.

10 ... Bb4

Sharp and unusual. Nor-

mal is 10 ... Be7.
11 cxd5 exd5 12 Bd3 d4 13 0-0 Bxc3 14 Nc4 Qh5 15 bxc3 Nd5 16 Bg3 dxe3 17 Rae1 Be6 18 fxe3 Rad8 19 Nd6 Ne5

20 Bxh7+

This is a new move. Previously seen here were 20 Nxb7 which led to a draw in the game Korchnoi - Lutz, Zurich 1999 and 20 Bf5 which ended up as a win for Black in the game Tukmakov - Lputian, Tilburg 1994.

20 ... Qxh7 21 Qxh7+ Kxh7 22 Bxe5 f6

The upshot of the combination is that White has won a pawn. However, his own pawns remain scat-

tered and with opposite bishops on the board a draw does not seem unlikely.

23 e4 Nb6

If 23 ... fxe5 24 Rxf8 Rxf8 25 exd5 Bxd5 26 Rxe5 with an extra pawn. However, in view of the game continuation it seems that this might have been Black's best chance for a draw, e.g. 26 ... Bc6 27 Re7 Rd8 28 Nxb7 Rd2 with counterplay.

24 Bg3 Na4 25 e5 f5 26 Bh4 Rd7 27 Re3 f4 28 Ref3 Bd5 29 Rh3 Be6 30 Be7+ Bxh3 31 Bxf8 Be6 32 Ne4 Kg8 33 Ng5 Kxf8 34 Nxe6+ Ke7 35 Nxf4 Rd2 36 Rf3

With White having two extra pawns his victory is no longer in doubt.

36 ... Nc5 37 h4 Ne6 38 Kh2 Ra2 39 Nxe6 Kxe6 40 Rg3 Kf7 41 e6+ Kxe6 42 Rxg7 Rxa3 43 Rxb7 Kf5 44 Rb5+ Kg4 45 Rb4+ Kh5 46 g3 Ra1 47 Kh3 a5 48 g4+ Kh6 49 Rb6+ Kg7 50 h5 a4 51 Ra6 a3 52 Kh4 a2 53 Kg5 Kh7 54 Ra7+ Kg8 55 Kg6 Kf8 56 g5 **Black resigns**

The Times *is one of very few papers to post the chess column on-line*

Chess Problems and Studies

Chess Problems (both composing and solving) and the related area of endgame studies is a bit of a specialist area, with its own history and even vocabulary. It is precisely in this type of subject where the Internet can come into its own. Not only can you find links to sites on the subjects, but also you can use it to make contacts if you're keen to take it further. You may just want to find some problems to entertain you or perhaps you want to enter composing or solving competitions. I doubt the Internet will replace the magazines and books devoted to this subject, but this could happen, and certainly it can be a starting place.

The International Chess Federation FIDE has what is known as its 'Permanent FIDE Commission for Chess Compositions', which has an unofficial website created by Hannu Harkola of Finland. You can see this website at
http://www.saunalahti.fi/~stniekat/pccc/index.htm.

The BDS website by Brian Stephenson is the home for the British Chess Solving Championship (which he runs) and the British Chess Problem Society (including information on how to join and about it's magazine *The Problemist*) in particular and chess problems in general also. It also has a links page to some other places of interest (including the slightly mocking chess player's view of a problem: 'Graham Brown invites you to make

THE MOST STUPID MOVE' **http://www.khcc.org.uk/gb.htm**).

The BDS site gives a number of links to individual problemists. Also it links to probably the most interesting of the pages on problems on the Internet at the moment. Solving Chess by Lubomir Siran is dedicated to chess solving, with results, a calendar of events and gradings. This can be seen at **http://geocities.com/solvingchess**. There is a wealth of material on solving here including timed exercises. It also has a very concentrated page of links to other solving sites at **http://geocities.com/solvingchess/links.html**. This whole site is probably the best starting place I found on this subject.

Other possible starting places are Vaclav Kotesovec's page, which has many problem links (but is in Czech) at **http://web.telecom.cz/vaclav.kotesovec** and also at **http://www.internetchess.com/problems.shtml**. This last site points to Chess Composition Books: Electronic editions of public domain works by Anders Thulin at **http://www.algonet.se/~ath**. This site has a number of free electronic books for you to download. On the same kind of theme he recommends Problemiste Matthieu Leschemelle's Shareware program for checking problems which is available at **http://perso.easynet.fr/~mleschen/prb/problem.htm**; this also has a large number of problems for download.

It is always worth following up links specifically given from specialist sites as they often lead to hidden gems. Another site where you can download problems is Chess Problems Archive which is at **http://gpnm.iquebec.com/gpnm** (it is in French).

Reference and Contacts

If you were to look at it numerically, I suppose the largest number of chess related sites on the Internet are in this category of reference and contact. Indeed, this is as it should be. Every organisation, tournament, author, player and so on ought to consider having a website. These kinds of informational websites don't have to be very sophisticated. Their purpose is to answer common queries, promote a tournament for which you want entries and give contact details such as email, telephone and mail addresses, so that people who need to get in contact or would like some specific information can find it.

Promoting Tournaments, the Easy Way

I receive a lot of email which promote tournaments. Some are huge messages with word processor documents attached and they are sent to a large number of people. This is both inefficient and a little bit rude to those unfortunate to find themselves on a mailing list to which they don't want to belong (I don't mind – it's my job). A better approach if you wish to get entries and publicity for an event is to compose a short email with the basic details: dates, place, contact and website address. Leave the website to carry the strain of the minute detail. It also means it's much easier for other websites to carry this basic information, something less likely to happen if a huge document has to be boiled down to its basic detail.

A number of organisers work hard to promote their tournaments. In Hungary the capital Budapest is host to the First Saturday Chess Tournaments, organised by Laszlo Nagy almost every month. He has a basic contact website at **http://www.elender.hu/~firstsat**. These are amongst the most successful norm tournaments, that is events where there are entry fees for players seeking international experience and the possibility of IM and GM norms – they are matched with the correct strength of opposition to make these norms possible. Nagy's events have run for many years and he's even started to run events elsewhere, such as in Yugoslavia. Although they occur less frequently, chess organiser Adam Raoof runs events along the same lines in the UK. His Chess Circuit page is at **http://www.circuit.demon.co.uk**.

Federation Sites and Regional Sites

Chess federation and regional sites can serve a number of different purposes. Their first and prime reason for existing is so people who need to get in contact with the Federation can do so. They should also, if possible, carry the decisions, press releases, tournament calendars and perhaps even ratings under their control. If their purpose is more ambitious they should also promote chess in their region. Many Federation and Regional sites provide internet coverage of their national championships and even offer their space to cover the more important events happening in their country. There is a vast range of quality and investment in websites in this area.

As mentioned before, some federation sites concentrate on giving information to their own members. An example of this would be the Spanish Chess Federation (**http://www.feda.org**) who have a nicely designed site with regulations, contacts, addresses, tournament calendar and so forth. This is quite similar to the British Chess Federation (**http://www.bcf.ndirect.co.uk**) and the Scottish Chess Association (**http://www.users.globalnet.co.uk/%7Esca/sca.htm**). The Yugoslav Chess Federation at **http://sah.vrsac.com** do this but they also present general chess news in Yugoslavian which is not widely catered for on the Internet (although respected Yugoslav journalist Sinisa Joksic has started a site of news at: **http://avala.yubc.net/~yuchess**). There comes a point where a Federation site moves from being a purely administrative information site into something more and the boundaries, especially with chess news, become blurred. The Dutch Chess Federation's site at **http://www.schaakbond.nl** is a mixture of news and admin information written in Dutch. Many of the best sites promote their own chess to their country and also to abroad. The Australian Chess Federation (**http://www.auschess.org.au**) not only promotes its own events; it also covers those of its region. You can read about International Chess in Oceania at: **http://www.auschess.org.au/oceania.**

The Estonian Chess Federation (**http://www.online.ee/~maleliit**) has basic news from the Estonian chess scene in three languages, Estonian, English and Spanish. Their purpose is to promote to wider audience events involving their players. There are some countries where it is very hard to get information from except from the official website. The Armenian Chess Federation **http://www.armchess.am** has brief contact information but its main point of interest for the outsider is that it covers their national championships and most important other events such as zonals and World Junior Championships. This is a very accurate site, with the games from the events they cover always being very well produced. My only criticism is their insistence on using graphics instead of html for almost all the written material apart from the games.

Chess Sector (Ukrainian Chess Online) **http://chess-sector.odessa.ua** is without doubt the best source of information on chess in the Ukraine. Written in both Russian and English, it promotes Ukrainian chess and in particular its young star in the making Ruslan Ponomariov. It is always an indication that a regional site is interested in promoting their chess to an international audience when you see them in more than the host language, such as with the Estonian and Ukrainian sites (interestingly I know of no English speaking site with sections written in a foreign language).

To fund a website which has more than basic ambitions requires money, so there are more commercial websites. The French Chess Association signed a deal with Kasparovchess.com over their website at **http://www.echecs.asso.fr**, so most of its design stems from Kasparovchess. The Brazilian Chess Federation (**http://www.cbx.org.br**) covers live or daily many of the events in the region as well as major events further afield and also takes advertising. The United States Chess Federation (**http://www.uschess.org**) has always had a commercial element to it, including a site called **http://www.uschesslive.org** and a chess shop.

The International Chess Federation FIDE (**http://www.fide.com**) itself has signed over many of its potential money making activities to a separate company called FIDE Commerce. They have quite a bit of shopping and advertising. However, in terms of basic information about the organisation they are not lacking either. You should at least become familiar with its contents.

Their website has several sections:

Firstly, the News and Events section, of which by far the most important is the Press Releases section. Here some of the most important FIDE documents are published. They also have a Calendar of FIDE events and a Chess Review (which seems not to have been updated for a little while and at one time lifted many results from TWIC).

Secondly, there's the Database section of players, federations (very useful for lists of federation sites and contact numbers), commissions, arbiters, title applications (you can check for new titled players), ratings (extremely important database of all FIDE rated players) and games archives (mostly of previous FIDE events).

Thirdly, the Official Info section has the FIDE Handbook (an incredible resource which includes amongst other things the official rules of chess), lists of officials and Honorary Members.

The final part is their services section which they're hoping to build upon greatly. They have a virtually empty Game Zone that may become very important if, as projected, official FIDE internet events take place, their Chess Links, Top Chess Sites and Banner Exchange program which is a pretty interesting commercial venture for them. Finally they have a shop for many chess goods.

Chess Clubs

Much of what I've said about federation sites can also apply to chess club sites. These can be very simple affairs, with just contact details and information about when the club meets, or something far more. There are some very prestigious clubs with websites on the Internet. The famous New York chess clubs, the Marshall Chess Club (**http://www.marshallchessclub.org**) and the Manhattan Chess Club (**http://www.manhattanchessclub.com**) both have sites which are about club news and events, the Manhattan Club also having some articles by Grandmaster Joel Benjamin. On the other coast the Mechanics' Institute in San Francisco (**http://www.chessclub.org**) is very active at the moment. GM John Donaldson produces a regular and worthwhile newsletter and they also cover the events, some of which are quite strong, hosted by the club. Often the enthusiasm and level of activity in a club is reflected in the website. A site like the Arlington Chess Club site (**http://www.wizard.net/~matkins**) gains in importance because one of its members (Michael Atkins) is a tournament director in many strong opens in the US. He often provides results and games from these events which otherwise wouldn't be seen.

Large and thriving clubs often have websites that are interesting and worth visiting in their own right. Hull Chess Club (**http://www.hullchessclub.karoo.net**), Barnet (**http://www.gtryfon.demon.co.uk/bcc**) and Kings Head Chess Club in London (**http://www.khcc.org.uk**) are English sites with not only news and features about the club itself, but also articles of general interest.

A number of European chess clubs are the host to very strong events which they cover on their web pages. In the last year Bundesliga clubs such as Lübecker Schachverein 1873 (**http://www.lsv1873.de**) have started providing coverage of their own matches from what is still the strongest national league in the World. Perhaps the most striking success is that of the Frankfurt-West Chess Club (**http://www.frankfurt-west.de**). Their rapidplay chess event has been without doubt the strongest ever. The President of the club Hans-Walter Schmitt has somehow managed to strengthen the event year by year, with the top ten players in the World participating in various events during the tournament of 2000. In fact, the only plan I've heard him mention that seems not to have come to fruition was to get Bobby Fischer to play.

Cannes Chess Club (**http://www.cannes-echecs.org**) is another club site with a fine tradition of strong events. For the last couple of years they have held regular matches involving Vladislav Tkachiev, and this year (2001) they're one of the host sites for the World Rapidplay Cup which involves Garry Kasparov amongst others in a strong field.

It's simply not possible to either keep track of or list all the clubs on the Internet. However, if you are looking for somewhere to play, most major cities or areas have some information available.

Computer Chess

Computers and the Internet go hand in hand. Therefore it should not be a great surprise that material on chess playing programs and chess software in general should be well covered on the Internet. I've mentioned various computer software sites at various points during the book. Here I'm talking about interesting sites, where the main subject is computer chess. If you're a budding programmer you can get code and advice for any number of chess tasks. If you're interested how a program performs against other programs or professional players, or even would like to hear the opinions of, or get in touch with, professional programmers, the Internet is the place to do it.

For many years the newsgroups saw many of the major figures in computer chess contribute to discussions. There is a newsgroup devoted to this subject still; it is called rec.games.chess.computer. However, discussion became very heated there at times and a number of the leading programmers decided a more moderated forum was appropriate. They set up the Computer Chess Club (**http://www.icdchess.com**). This forum still allows open posting of your views, but because it requires registration it means that there is some sanction against inflammatory posting. Nevertheless, there are some pretty frank exchanges of view along with exceptionally interesting information and tips.

The International Computer Chess Association (**http://www.dcs.qmw.ac.uk/~icca**), which holds amongst other things the Microcomputer Chess Championships, has a basic site but does have a solid links page at **http://www.dcs.qmw.ac.uk/~icca/cc_links.htm**, including links to a couple of articles on chess programming by Dr A. N. Walker (**http://www.maths.nott.ac.uk/personal/anw/G13GT1/compch.html**) and to a page by Paul Verhelst (**http://www.xs4all.nl/~verhelst/chess/programming.html**), although this seems somewhat dated and some of the links no longer work.

The Swedish Chess Computer Association (**http://home.swipnet.se/~w-36794/ssdf**) is an independent organisation for people interested in chess computers and computer software related to chess. Its rating list for chess playing programs is the most important and influential one as they don't allow commercial interference in its production.

Germany seems to be very keen on computer chess, with a number of sites wholly or dominantly in German. Frank Quisinsky's computer chess pages at **http://amateurschach.in-trier.de** give links to free and commercial computer chess playing programs and a strong and well maintained links list. Gambit soft (**http://www.gambitsoft.com**) is a commercial site which sells computer products but also has a lot of chess computer related material including Komputer Korner (**http://www.gambitsoft.com/komputer.htm**). This reviews various aspects of computer software, including tips on how to produce your own opening books. The magazine **http://www.computerschach.de** also has a number of important resources.

If you're interested in Deep Blue then IBM's site for the match in 1997 when it beat Kasparov 3½-2½ is still around at **http://www.research.ibm.com/deepblue**. One of the great names in computing as a whole as well as computer chess is Ken Thompson, who has a homepage at **http://cm.bell-labs.com/who/ken/index.html**.

Correspondence Chess

The advent of strong chess playing computers might be thought to spell the death knell for correspondence chess. It hasn't proved to be the case and what is more, the Internet has probably guaranteed its future for some time. The vast majority of games played online are blitz games, so what do you do if you want to play a serious game? Perhaps the answer might be correspondence chess. The correspondence game, as played by normal mail, has started to converge with that played by email. The International Correspondence Chess Federation (ICCF – **http://www.iccf.com)** was a little slow off the mark in this respect. They have only just started their first email World Chess Championship, which is taking place at the time of writing. Their site is full of information about the Federation and correspondence chess in general. There were others who were quicker to recognise the potential for correspondence chess via the Internet. Tim Harding was an early enthusiast and his Chess Mail magazine (**http://www.chessmail.com**) is one of the biggest advocates for correspondence chess in all its forms. A website with book reviews, features, links and articles compliment his excellent printed magazine.

Another advocate is correspondencechess.com (**http://www.correspondencechess.com**). John C. Knudsen runs the whole site, but he has a number of contributors who produce their own mini-sites within his main site. Elements include:

The Correspondence Chess Place by Knudsen himself looks at many issues surrounding correspondence chess (CC), including how to get started, avoiding mistakes, computer use in CC, an annotated set of links and an archive of 180,000 games.

The Campbell report by Franklin Campbell, who is one of the best writers on correspondence chess. He has articles, news, live coverage, links, cross tables and more.

Other mini-sites include:

Victor Palciauskas 10th World Correspondence Chess Champion
Ralph Marconi's Chess Pages
The Official ICCF On-Line Game Archive
The Canadian Correspondence Chess Association
American Postal Chess Tournaments
Chess Journalists of America
The Correspondence Chess Message Board
Correspondence Chess News

All in all this and Chess Mail are must visit sites for correspondence chess players and contain much more general interest as well.

As the ICCF was slow to accept correspondence chess by email, the vacuum was filled by the International Email Chess Group (IECG – **http://www.iecg.org**). Many of the same players who play serious correspondence chess under the aegis of the ICCF also play in IECG events. Playing by email has two advantages:

1) Delivery time

2) No postage costs.

One of the objections has been that verifying when moves have been sent and received via email is difficult, but that seems to have been overcome. The IECG hold events for all strengths of player and have their own qualification and World Championship system. It is now a highly organised and important body in the correspondence chess world.

Other correspondence chess sites

The US office of the ICCF has a separate site at **http://www.iccfus.com**. Another site of interest is the British Correspondence Chess Association (**http://www.dbsugden.clara.net**).

The International Email Chess Club IECC website is at **http://www.geocities.com/Colosseum/Midfield/1264**, which is a little more friendly in its competition.

The Gambitchess site at **http://www.gambitchess.com** also offers email chess; especially interesting are its thematic openings events.

The Internet Chess Tournaments site at: **http://chess.webest.com** is a way to play correspondence chess using a web interface rather than email.

My thanks to Martin Bennedik for his recommendations in this area.

Chess Teaching

There are a huge number of chess teaching and coaching sites. Many simply advertise the services of competent (or perhaps not) trainers and of titled players. The Internet certainly opens up the possibility of distance learning in the future, with your favourite Grandmaster if you have the money to do it. Already on ICC I believe some Grandmasters offer lessons or games that you can pay for on-line, the quality I imagine will be entirely down to the player involved.

Maurice Ashley and Michael Rohde have pay per view lectures at the ChessWise site at **http://www.chesswise.com**; in addition you can see some free material. The KasparovChess University intended to plug into a similar market and there are a number of pay per view multimedia exercises at **http://www.kasparovchess.com**. it's not clear how successful it has been at getting subscribers but I've no doubt the time will eventually come for this.

Beginners Chess

There are coaching and beginners resources on the Internet. If you're an absolute beginner and want to learn the rules I would sincerely suggest buying one of the many excellent primers that have been published over the years. Nevertheless, there are worthwhile resources out there. I will give three sites that should be good enough for most beginners needs.

The Exeter Chess Club Coaching Page (**http://info.ex.ac.uk/~dregis/DR/coaching.html**) is one of the most well known pages for coaching resources and deservedly so. It has a huge number of exercises and links to other sites and should be the starting point for any investigation of this subject.

365 Chess Lessons at **http://www.xmission.com/~vote/365/index.htm** has a chess lesson for every day of the year and includes an explanation of the rules of the game.

About.com **http://chess.about.com** has sections on how to play, beginners and improve your game (all links on the left hand side).

Other Sites for Beginners

There is an interesting site at **http://www.chesstrainer.com,** advertising the Euwe Chess Academy in India. It has an explanation of the rules of the game and some elementary tactics exercises. ChessPro.com (**http://www.chesspro.com**) is a similar type of site; it has a number of free exercises and an explanation of chess notation and PGN which novices might find useful. Claude Kaber's Homepage at **http://webplaza.pt.lu/public/ckaber/index.html** has a set of training exercises you can download and use.

Chess Openings

One of the things about the Internet is that although games are free, annotated and written material is copyrighted. Chess openings is an area of expertise and in general; the stronger the player the better the material can be. There is some free material: pure game collections such as the La Regence site, where recent games are arranged by opening (**http://www.notzai.com/notzai/regence/regence.shtml**) and enthusiasts sites such as 1 b4 is a winning opening (**http://www.sokolski.de/indexg.htm**), the Winckelmann-Reimer Gambit home page (**http://home.mira.net/~fludy**) and the Gambit Experts site (**http://www.thomasstock.com/gambit/expert.htm**). However, there is perhaps less on the Internet than might be expected.

There is one highly interesting site which you have to pay to use. This is Chris White's Chess Publishing (**http://www.chesspublishing.com**). He has a number of experts, with titled players Tony Kosten, Paul Motwani, John Emms, Andrew Martin, Aaron Summerscale, Ruslan Sherbakov, Alexander Volzhin, Gary Lane, John Fedorowicz, Chris Ward and Neil McDonald writing for the site in the different specialist areas. The site was reviewed by John Watson at (**http://www.chesscenter.com/twic/jwatson18.html**), his basic conclusion being that it's worth it, but only if you have a basic chess playing strength. This site may eventually be the model for more serious pay per view content on the Internet; at the moment it certainly is almost unique.

Link and Guide Sites

If I achieve anything in writing this book I hope for one thing; that it will get you up and running on the Internet and capable in finding what you need, when you need it, and be confident in doing that. Everyone has their own web favourites and beyond a core few sites there are often many alternatives for finding information you might want. I have my view and that is what you are reading in this book, but hopefully I'll be able to impart enough knowledge for you to find what you want and make your own mind up. I mentioned earlier about search engines and how to use them. However, they sometimes aren't the best way of finding sites. Web directories and guides (a little like this book, except on the Internet) are a key part of finding your way around.

There are two parts to producing a web guide. First of all, how comprehensive is it? A comprehensive site of links is extremely useful, but on the other hand, thirty thought out links might be better!

Secondly, are they regularly updated? I don't want to find that most of the sites linked have either moved or no longer exist and I do want to know about sites that have just started up. For this book I checked every single page to see whether they were still there or if there was a more up to date link. Sites I quote with addresses starting with things like **http://www.geocities.com**, **http://ourworld.compuserve.com** and **http://webhome.globalserve.net** are hobby sites hosted by commercial companies; they are vulnerable as addresses because their writers may find a better deal elsewhere and move the sites. This also applies to sites set up by students or staff at Universities; they could change job. Those who have registered their own site names can change the computer they use to host the website without changing address. Keeping up to date with the changes is a big job and new websites take some time to get a base of people visiting.

There have been many web directories over the years; many have fallen by the wayside or haven't been updated in two or three years. In fact, often people compile a very good links page once and then never touch it again. It's a very time sensitive area.

About.com is a site worth knowing even if you don't plan to use it for chess. They have personal guides to the Internet on over 700 subjects. The chess section, edited by David Dunbar, is one of the best (**http://chess.about.com**). Subjects they promise to cover include Rules: How to Play, Beginners, Improve Your Game, Play on the Net, Chat & Interviews, Chess For Fun, Clubs, Databases, Endgames, Bobby Fischer, History, Reviews, Garry Kasparov, Magazines/Columns, Newsgroups, Openings, Organizations, Postal Chess, Puzzles, Scholastic Chess, Shopping, Players, Software, Tournaments, Trivia, Variants and World Champions. The site has specially written articles on major subjects and links to much more; they also have a lively discussion forum. They keep articles going back quite some time and this is probably a mixed blessing. It does mean that they have a huge body of material but a slight criticism is that some of it could do with being updated more frequently. They are especially strong in their coverage of sites that have been a fixture for some time. As I've said before, my main gripe with the site is that about.com's links are done in such a way that you have the about.com logo and address at the top of the page. it's sometimes hard to establish which website they're linking to. This is a horrid practice but it is their standard. That aside, there is no question this is a place you should visit often and bookmark.

It was hard to know where to place Alan Cowderoy's Palamede site in the book. It's a collection of major non-profit websites that work together. The homepage at **http://www.palamede.com** contains links to the different sites and parts of those sites, and to current events. It also has its own chess calendar of events (**http://www.palamede.com/cgi-bin/calendar/calendar.pl**) and chess javascript viewer (**http://www.enpassant.dk/chess/palview/index.htm**). The sites that make up the co-operation are:

En passant by Eric Bentzen (**http://www.enpassant.dk**). This is a World reference site for chess publishing software and utilities and home to Norresundby Chess Club.
Chess Graphics (**http://www.cowderoy.com/graphics/index.htm**) – the largest collection of chess graphics on the net.
Chess Variants by Hans Bodlaender and David Smith at **http://www.chessvariants.com**, a reference site for variant forms of the game.

Notzai by Pascal Villalba at **http://www.notzai.com**. This is a French language news site on the web.

La Regence (**http://www.notzai.com/notzai/regence/index.shtml**) – a database of recent games sorted by eco code.

Mieux Jouer aux Echecs by Reyes at **http://www.mjae.com**, an educational site in French.

There is no question that the site: **http://www.internetchess.com** was one of the leading links site at one time. It still has a huge number of links to many websites. It is now owned by braingames.net but even before that it was starting to look a little under administered and the number of dead links to pages long gone is rather large.

One of the more clever ideas is the FIDE banner network available at **http://www.fide.com**. Their chess banner network produces a ranking of websites at **http://counter.fide.com**. Of course FIDE gain by getting website figures for a whole range of sites, which is why many of the major chess sites on the Internet have not joined. For a small or moderately sized site it worth considering as a way to promote your site. The lists of sites give a good idea of which sites are active or appreciated and is one good place to investigate the Internet for a chess subject you are interested in.

A site with a huge (perhaps the largest) list of categorised links is the famous magazine New in Chess **http://www.newinchess.com**. With such a huge number of sites it must be hard to administer but it is probably the major links page today.

Chessopolis Essential Links Page is available at **http://www.chessopolis.com/essential.htm**. From there you can browse chess related websites by category from a menu on the left hand side.

Ben Hummel's chess links in Dutch at **http://schaak.startplaza.nl** has a good selection of well maintained links to all sorts of chess related websites.

MSO World have a links page **http://www.msoworld.com/links/pages/index.html**, which includes a big number of chess related links.

Its always worth mentioning Steve Pribut's Chess Page at **http://www.clark.net/pub/pribut/chess.html**, not only is it the site of the chess FAQ but also he has a number of good, if old, links.

Chapter Seven

Index of Chess Sites

Chess Auctions

Chess Auctions on-line **http://chessauction.tripod.com/**
Salesbid and Chess & Bridge Auction site **http://www.salesbid.com/partners/chess/**

Chess Book and Software Reviews

Allan Savage's reviews for Chess Mail **http://www.chessmail.com/savage_review.html**
Chess Café Book Reviews by Taylor Kingston
http://www.chesscafe.com/REVIEWS/books.HTM
Chess Program Reviews **http://www.chessreviews.com/**
Chessopolis **http://www.chessopolis.com/**
Jeremy Silman's Book reviews for Inside Chess **http://www.insidechess.com./silman.html**
John Elburg's Chessbookreviews Homepage **http://www.chessmail.com/books/**
John Watson's Book Reviews **http://www.chesscenter.com/twic/watson.html**
Randy's Revealing Reviews **http://ourworld.compuserve.com/homepages/randybauer/**
Stephen Leary reviews at MSO World **http://www.msoworld.com/**
Tim Harding's review for Chess Mail **http://www.chessmail.com/reviews.html**

Chess Bulletin Boards

About.com Chess Bulletin Board **http://forums.about.com/ab-chess/start/**
Bulletin Board **http://f11.parsimony.net/forum16635/**
Chess Café Bulletin Board **http://www.chesscafe.com/board/board.htm**
Computer Chess Club **http://www.icdchess.com/**
Yahoo Clubs: Chess History **http://clubs.yahoo.com/clubs/chesshistory**

Chess Calendar

Palmede Chess Calendar **http://www.palamede.com/cgi-bin/calendar/calendar.pl**

Chess Club

Aalborg Skakforening **http://www.business.auc.dk/~gv/chess/**
Arlington Chess Club **http://www.wizard.net/~matkins/**
Barnet Chess Club **http://www.gtryfon.demon.co.uk/bcc/**
Bergen Chess Club **http://home.online.no/~eirikgu/bs.htm**
Chess Life. LJCDS and Diegueno Country School Chess Club Page. **http://chesslife.com/**
Club de Ajedrez la Expansión de Hortaleza **http://www.terra.es/personal/8g2doem8623/**
Collado Villalba Chess Club **http://www.terra.es/personal2/c.a.c.v/**
Edinburgh University Chess Club **http://www.ed.ac.uk/~chess/**
Foment Martinenc Chess Club from Barcelona **http://www.terra.es/personal2/cefoment/**
Kings Head Chess Club **http://www.khcc.org.uk/**
Koninklijke Gentse Schaakkring Ruy Lopez **http://www.kgsrl.be/**
LASK Chess Club **http://lask.schacknyheter.com/**
Lübecker Schachverein 1873 **http://www.lsv1873.de/**
Manhatten Chess Club **http://www.manhattanchessclub.com/**
Marshall Chess Club **http://www.marshallchessclub.org/**
Mechanics Institute **http://www.milibrary.org/**
Mechanic's Institute Chess Club **http://www.chessclub.org/**
Official website of the Hamburger SK von 1830 e.V. **http://www.hsk1830.de/**
Pittsburgh Chess Club **http://trfn.clpgh.org/pcc/index.html**
Portland Chess Institute **http://www.portlandchess.com/**
Rochade Kuppenheim **http://www.rochadekuppenheim.de/**
Schaakliga Limburg VZW **http://www.geocities.com/limliga/**
Schachfreunde 1982 Baiertal-Schatthausen e.V. **http://www.sf-baiertal.de**
Schachklub Turm Emsdetten e.V. **http://www.deltacity.net/michael/**
SF Katernberg **http://www.sfk-schach.de/**
South Birmingham Chess Club **http://sbcc.members.beeb.net/home.html**
Sutton Coldfield Chess Club **http://www.brum2000.swinternet.co.uk/**
Taastrup Skakforening (Danish Chessclub) **http://home3.inet.tele.dk/kbv/**
Three Cs chess club **http://www.btinternet.com/~threecs.chess/**
Wessex Chess Club **http://www.users.globalnet.co.uk/~mjyeo/wessex.htm**
Wyoming and Cheyenne Chess Page **http://members.aol.com/DDDJon/wyoming-chess.html**
Zeno club of Glyfada **http://users.forthnet.gr/ath/zinon/**

Chess Coaching and Training

365 Chess Lessons **http://www.xmission.com/~vote/365/index.htm**

Ajedrez Hoy: Chess School. http://ajedrezhoy.com/

Association Échecs et Maths http://www.echecs.org/

Barnet Chess Club Beginners tips
http://www.chessclub.demon.co.uk/tutorial/learning/learning.htm

Chess Academy of Canada http://www3.sympatico.ca/chessacademycanada/

Chess Doctor http://chessdoctor.com

Chess in the Schools, tournaments page. http://members.aol.com/chiachess/

ChessKids Academy http://www.chesskids.com/

Chess'n Math Association http://www.chess-math.org/

ChessTrainer.com http://www.chesstrainer.com/

Chesstraining - Claude Kaber's Homepage http://webplaza.pt.lu/public/ckaber/index.html

Chessweb http://www.chesspro.com/

Chesswise University http://www.chesswise.com/

Claude Kaber - Homepage http://webplaza.pt.lu/public/ckaber/Mainpage.htm

Correspondence player Jon Edwards page.
http://www.princeton.edu/~jedwards/cif/intro.html

Deutsche Schachjugend (DSJ) http://Deutsche-Schachjugend.de/dsj

die-schachaufgabe.de http://www.die-schachaufgabe.de/

Dorobanov International http://www.dorobanov.com/

Exeter Chess Club Coaching Page http://info.ex.ac.uk/~dregis/DR/coaching.html

Gregory Kaidanov's chess pages. http://members.iglou.com/kaidanov/

IM Eric Tangborn's site http://www.geocities.com/eric_98008/index.html

Internet Chess Academy with Gabriel Schwartzman http://www.totalchess.com/

Jamaican Ambassadors Chess Academy http://jambassadors.virtualave.net/newfile.html

Jussupow Schachakademie
http://ourworld.compuserve.com/homepages/Artur_Jussupow/

Justin Morris's page http://www.kidchess.com/

Kaidanov's Coaching Page http://kaidanov.8m.com/

Mieux Jouer aux Echecs by Reyes http://www.mjae.com/

NM Dan Heisman's Chess Page http://members.home.net/danheisman/chess.htm

NJ PRØBLEMsm Chess Services http://www.noproblemcs.com/chess.htm

Ponti Chess Club http://www.geocities.com/Colosseum/Track/7733/index.html

Portland Chess Institute http://www.portlandchess.com

Richmond Junior Chess Club http://www.rjcc.org.uk/

RookKnightRook http://www.geocities.com/rookknightrook/index.html

Schachakademie Holger Möller http://www.schachakademie.com

Schachtraining On-line with Bernd Rosen http://home.t-online.de/home/LuckyBaer/

Stichting Bevorderen Schaken Apeldoorn http://www.sbsa.nl/

US Chess Center http://www.chessctr.org/home.htm

Western PA Youth Chess Homepage http://trfn.clpgh.org/pcc/youth.htm

Chess Events and Organisers

1st World Chess Cup in China **http://www.worldchesscup.com**
Annual Voronezh Chess Open **http://www.relex.ru/~xuser/voronezh_open/**
Continental Chess Association **http://www.chesstour.com/**
Dutton Chess **http://www.play.at/duttonchess**
First Saturday Chess in Hungary (Laszlo Nagy) **http://www.elender.hu/~firstsat**
World Open **http://www.worldopen.com**

Chess FAQ

FAQ it.hobby.scacchi **http://www.pi.infn.it/~carosi/ihs.html**
Steve Pribut's Chess Page **http://www.clark.net/pub/pribut/chess.html**

Chess Federation

Ajedrez en Costa Rican Chess **http://ns.racsa.co.cr/ajedrez/**
Armenian Chess Federation **http://www.armchess.am/**
Australian Chess Federation **http://www.auschess.org.au/**
Austrian Chess Federation **http://www.chess.at/**
Belgian Chess Federation **http://www.ping.be/dwarrelwind/kbsb/**
Bermuda Chess Association **http://www.bermuda.bm/chess/**
Brazilian Chess Federation **http://www.cbx.org.br/**
British Chess Federation **http://www.bcf.ndirect.co.uk/**
Bulgarian Chess Federation **http://hades.bsc.bg/6wstudch/bcf.htm**
Canadian Chess Federation **http://www.chess.ca/**
Croatian Chess Federation **http://www.crochess.com/**
Czech Chess Federation **http://www.chess.cz/**
Danish Chess Federation **http://www.dsu.dk/**
Deutscher Schachbund (DSB) **http://www.schachbund.de/**
Dutch Chess Federation **http://www.schaakbond.nl/**
Estonian Chess Federation **http://www.online.ee/~maleliit/**
Faroese Chess Federation **http://www.faroechess.com/**
FIDE site. **http://www.fide.com/**
French Chess Federation **http://www.echecs.asso.fr/**
Hungarian Chess Federation **http://www.chess.hu/**
Israeli Chess Federation **http://www.chess.org.il/**
Italian Chess Federation **http://www.infcom.it/fsi/**
Korean Chess Federation **http://www.koreachess.org/**
La Fédération Monégasque des Echecs **http://www.multimania.com/fme/fme/fme.htm**
Lebanese Chess Federation **http://www.lebchess.org**
Macau Chess Association **http://www.unitel.net/chessmacau/**
Mexican Chess Federation **http://www.galeon.com/fenamac/**

Norwegian Chess Federation **http://www.sjakk.no/**
Pakistan Chess Player **http://pakchess.cjb.net/**
Paraguay Chess Federation **http://www.quanta.com.py/feparaj/index.htm**
Polish Chess Federation **http://www.pzszach.org.pl/**
Puerto Rican Chess **http://php.indiana.edu/%7Ejsoto/PURaje.html**
Republic of Panama Chess Federation **http://www.ciudadfutura.com/superajedrez/fenap/**
Scottish Chess Federation **http://www.users.globalnet.co.uk/%7Esca/sca.htm**
Slovak Chess Federation **http://www.chess.sk/**
Slovenian Chess Federation **http://www.sah-zveza.si/**
Spanish Chess Federation **http://www.feda.org/**
Swedish Chess Federation **http://www.schack.se/**
Swiss Chess Federation **http://www.schachbund.ch/**
Trinidad And Tobago Chess Association **http://www.caribchess.com/ttca.htm**
US Chess Federation **http://www.uschess.org/**
Yugoslav Chess Federation **http://sah.vrsac.com/**

Chess Games

Chess Wise Secret games from the chess masters
http://www.chesswise.com/world_games.htm
ChessBase On-Line **http://www.chessbase-online.com**
chess-international.de Die Schachadresse im Internet **http://www.chess-international.de/**
ChessLab **http://www.chesslab.com**
Downloadable chess-games around the internet **http://www.rhrk.uni-kl.de/~balzer/chessgames.html**
RusBase **http://www.ruschess.com/Rusbase/main.html**
Thomas Stock's Chess Site **http://www.ThomasStock.com/chessindex.html**
University of Pittsburgh Chess Page **http://www.pitt.edu/~schach**

Chess Games: National Game Databases

América-Base **http://www.ajedrez-de-estilo.com.ar/ade/jag/ambase/ambase.htm**
Argentine Base **http://www.geocities.com/Colosseum/Mound/7762/jag/base1.htm**
Britbase British Chess Game Archive **http://www.bcmchess.co.uk/britbase/**
CzechBase **http://www.fortunecity.com/olympia/chamberlain/316/**
Danbase **http://www.dsu.dk/partier/danbase.htm**
Dutchbase
http://www.maxeuwe.nl/frameset/frames2.cfm?page_id=bibliotheek1.cfm?paginanr=3
Finnish Chess Game Database **http://www.tpu.fi/~jarmo/suomipelit/**
ItalBase **http://members.tripod.com/~italbase/**
MontrealBase **http://132.206.45.67/chess/database.htm**
Polbase **http://www.republika.pl/polbase**
Polbase **http://repubIika.pl/polbase/**

Swebase http://svebas.schacknyheter.com/
UkrBase http://chess-sector.odessa.ua/ukrbase.html
Yubase http://user.tninet.se/~rhl458j/yubase/

Chess Hardware

Digital Game Timer Projects http://www.dgtprojects.com/

Chess History

Chess Goddesses Women in chess http://www.chessgoddesses.com/
On Nimzowitsch http://www.xs4all.nl/~wimnij/bio.html
The Game is Afoot. Chess History by Terry Crandall
http://www.pstat.ucsb.edu/~carlson/chess/
World Chess Championship http://www.mark-weeks.com/chess/wcc-indx.htm

Chess Interest

Onulet's Chess Pages http://www.jkronz.com/

Chess Lessons

Open Your Eyes (FM Akira Watanabe's site)
http://www.coara.or.jp/~koike/watanabe/index.htm

Chess Links

Ajedrez Informacion actual http://ajedrezactual.com/
Ben Hummel's chess links http://schaak.startplaza.nl/
Bobby Fischer Links http://www.chesslinks.org/hof/fischer.html
Chess Informant: Links http://www.sahovski.co.yu/flinks.htm
Chess Links http://www.rochadekuppenheim.de/links/index.html
Chess links in German http://www.meome.de/app/de/portal_bookmark.jsp/43139.html
Chess Space http://www.chess.imaginot.com/
Chess World http://www.very-best.de/ChessWorld.htm
Chessindex http://freespace.virgin.net/kenny.m/Chessindex/Chessindex.htm
Chessking: The Ultimate Chess Resource with a FREE Chess tutorial online!
http://www.chessking.com/
Chesslinks Worldwide http://www.chesslinks.org/
Chessopolis Essential Links Page http://www.chessopolis.com/essential.htm
Chesstimes http://www.chesstimes.org
Christopher Hodgins chess links page http://www.chodgins.f2s.com/
Finnish chess links http://www.funet.fi/pub/doc/games/chess/suomi/
Interactive Chess Links http://deltafarms.com/chess/

Internetchess.com **http://www.internetchess.com/**
Kaissa **http://www.geocities.com/Colosseum/Field/8203/**
Looksmart.com **http://www.looksmart.com/**
maro's Chess Page **http://www.geocities.com/CapeCanaveral/Launchpad/2640/chess.htm**
Meome chess by Erhard Frolik **http://www.meome.de/schach**
Noel Aldebol's Chess Site **http://sites.netscape.net/nycdbol/chess**
Pakistan Chess Player **http://pakchess.paklinks.com/**
schaak.pagina.nl **http://schaak.pagina.nl**
Schach-Web **http://www.schach-web.de**
Stefan's Schachseiten **http://www.chesspawn.de/**
Steve Pribut's Chess Page **http://www.clark.net/pub/pribut/chess.html**
The Chess Portal **http://mailer.fsu.edu/~Icabana/Chess.htm**
Turk Chess Education and Improvement Foundation **http://www.tursev.org.tr/**

Chess Links: Book Reviews

Schachverlag Kania: Book Reviews **http://www.kaniaverlag.de/htm/buchkatalog.html**

Chess Magazine

64 Chess Review. Home of the Chess Oscar. **http://www.64.ru/**
British Chess Magazine **http://www.bcmchess.co.uk**
Ceskoslovensky Sach **http://www.sach.cz/**
Chess and Bridge Site **http://www.chesscenter.com**
Chess in China **http://home.chinese.com/~chessinchina/**
Chess Informant **http://www.sahovski.com/**
Chess Mate **http://www.chess-mate.com/**
Chess Today **http://www.chesstoday.net/**
Electronic Xadrez site **http://www.exadrez.com.br**
Europe Echecs Magazein **http://www.europe-echecs.com**
Gambito **http://www.revistagambito.com/**
Inside Chess **http://www.insidechess.com**
Italia Scacchistica **http://maskeret.com/italiascacchistica/index.html**
Kaissiber **http://www.kaissiber.de/**
Kingpin **http://www.chesscenter.com/kingpin/Kingpin**
New in Chess **http://www.newinchess.com/**
Rochade Europa **http://ourworld.compuserve.com/homepages/rochade/**
Schach **http://www.zeitschriftschach.de/**
Schach Magazin 64 **http://www.schach-magazin.de**
Schachwoche **http://www.schach.ch/swinfo.htm**
The Australian Chess Forum **http://cs.anu.edu.au/~Shaun.Press/acforum.html**
Vistula Chess Monthly **http://www.astercity.net/~vistula**

Chess News

'Skakiera' (which means 'Chessboard') http://www.skakiera.gr/
1st Croatian Chess Home Page http://jagor.srce.hr/~davgolek
Adjedrez en Mexico http://aacevedo.tripod.com
Adrianroldan.com http://www.adrianroldan.com/
Agentura 64 Grygov http://www.proclient.cz/a64/
AjedreChess Multiweb http://ajedrez.hypermart.net/
Ajedrez Colombiano http://www5.gratisweb.com/ajedrezcolombia/
Ajedrez de Estilo http://www.ajedrez-de-estilo.com.ar/ade/
Ajedrez en Madrid http://www.ajedrezenmadrid.com/
Ajedrez en Mar del Plata http://members.nbci.com/jmacosta/
Ajedrez Noticias Diarias http://www.geocities.com/Yosemite/Falls/4480/betaclub.html
Ajedrez21 http://www.ajedrez21.com/
Ajedrezahoy http://ajedrezhoy.com.ar/
Annual Lausanne Young Masters http://www.lausanneyoungmasters.com/
Armenian Knight http://www.armenianknight.com/armchess/
Associação Cultural Luis de Camões http://www.terravista.pt/FerNoronha/3111/
Aydin Saray's Turkish Website http://e-satranc.8m.com/
Bavarian Chess http://members.aol.com/chessaround/chess/index.htm
Blackqueen.net http://www.blackqueen.net/
Bobby Ang's news from the Philippines. http://www.philchess.com.ph/
Brasilia Chess Club's Home Page http://www.persocom.com.br/bcx
Canalweb http://www.canalweb.com
Cannes-Echecs site http://www.cannes-echecs.org/
Chathurangam http://www.chathurangam.com/
Chess Circuit: Adam Raoof's Home Page http://www.circuit.demon.co.uk/
Chess in China http://cic.126.com
Chess in Iceland http://www.vks.is/skak/indexe.html
Chess Ireland http://www.iol.ie/~jghurley/
Chess Ireland http://ireland.iol.ie/~jghurley/
Chess News http://www.notzai.com/
Chess Sector (Ukrainian Chess Online) http://chess-sector.odessa.ua/
Chess Siberia http://www.chessib.com/
Chess Sixty Four http://www.64.net.cn/
Chess World Magazine http://www.fs2000.org/cwm/
Chessgate site http://www.chessgate.de
Chesslines http://www.chesslines.com
Chesswatch Site now part of Kasparovchess.com) http://www.kasparovchess.com/
Chessy Site http://www.chesslove.h1.ru/
Dutch Teletext http://teletekst.nos.nl/
Dutch Teletext chess page, no graphics http://teletekst.nos.nl/cgi-

bin/tt/nos/page/t/o/m/x/n/628-1

Echecs Province http://perso.wanadoo.fr/ermimaju/chess/echecs.html

Frankfurt-West Chess Club http://www.frankfurt-west.de/

Gerhard Hund's Teleschach pages. http://www.teleschach.de/

German Chess news site http://www.schachfreunde-buer.de/

GM Chess http://www.gmchess.com

GM-Schach http://www.gmschach.de

GREEK CHESS On Line @ OAA Heraklio Chess Club http://www.greekchess.com/

Guanjun Xiao's Chess in China site http://home.chinese.com/~chessinchina/

Hechtcer del Tablero http://www.hechiceros.net/

Hellas Chess Club http://www.chess.gr/

Hellir Chess Club http://simnet.is/hellir

Herman Claudius van Riemsdijk's Chess Page http://www.hipernet.com.br/HiperChess/

IBM site for Kasparov vs Deep Blue

http://www.research.ibm.com/deepblue/home/html/b.html

Infoxadrez. Luis Costa's chess site. http://www.infoxadrez.com

Innerschweizerischer Schachverband http://www.schach.ch/

International Chess in Oceania http://www.auschess.org.au/oceania/

Internet Chess Journal http://www.chessjournal.cz/

Irish Chess Archive http://www.markorr.net/tica/

Joe Black pages http://www.joeblack.h1.ru/

Jonathan Berry's homepage http://www.islandnet.com/~jberry/chess.htm

'JuegoCiencia. Todo el ajedrez. Un solo lugar' http://www.juegociencia.com.ar/

Kafejka Szachowa http://arrakis.put.poznan.pl/~piotrd/index.html

Kujawsko-Pomorski Zwiazek Szachowy http://www.szachy.lo.pl/

Lost Boys Site http://chess.lostcity.nl/

Luis Santos Homepage http://www.ip.pt/~ip001018/

Micio - Chess in Italy http://maskeret.com/micio/index.html

Miesiecznik Szachista http://www.szachista.home.pl/

Montreal Chess News by Hugh Brodie http://montrealchess.virtualave.net/

NDA http://www.come.to/NDA

NDA (Noticias de Ajedrez) http://www.fortunecity.com/olympia/hogan/1476/index.html

Net64 http://www.net64.es/

Net Chess News http://www.httpcity.com/ncn/

NZ Chess http://ourworld.compuserve.com/homepages/nzchess/

Quah Seng Sun's Malaysian Chess News http://chesscolumn.20m.com

Russian Chess http://www.ruschess.com

Russian site. Possibly FIDE's Elista office http://www.chessy.al.ru/

S3D Chess Online http://echess.dk.ru/

Šachový nárez http://www.karlin.mff.cuni.cz/~svatos/chess/sachy.htm

Scalise Chess Pages http://members.tripod.com/~scalise/

Schach Info und AnzeigenBörse http://www.schach-info.de

Schach.com http://www.schach.com
Schachseite der Wiener Zeitung http://schach.wienerzeitung.at/
ShakkiNet http://www.shakki.net/
Skakistiki Epikinonia Irakliou Attikis http://www.skaki.gr/
Something about chess http://kvkchess.euro.ru/
Something about chess http://kvkchess.boom.ru/
Sport Express http://www.sport-express.ru/
SuperAjedrez http://www.ciudadfutura.com/superajedrez/
TeleSchach http://teleschach.com
The Chess Oracle http://ourworld.compuserve.com/homepages/John_Katrin_Sharp/
The International Chessoid http://www.ticarchive.bizland.com/
The Week in Chess http://www.chesscenter.com/twic/twic.html
Uruwow.com chess site http://uruwow.com/secciones/deportes/ajedrez/
World Players Council Site http://ajedrez_democratico.tripod.com/
YU Chess (Sinisa Joksic) http://avala.yubc.net/~yuchess/

Chess Newsgroups

it.hobby.scacchi
maus.spiele.schach
nl.sport.schaken
gnu.chess
pdaxs.games.chess
rec.games.chess.analysis
rec.games.chess.computer
rec.games.chess.play-by-mail
fr.rec.jeux.echecs
rec.games.chess.politics
tw.bbs.rec.chess
zer.t-netz.schach
z-netz.alt.scach
rec.games.chess.misc
fido7.su.chess.play
free.uk.chess
fido7.su.chess
es.rec.juegos.ajedrez
de.alt.games.schach
chile.rec.deportes.ajedrez
alt.chess.ics
francom.echecs
Chess Newsgroup alt.chess.bdg

Chess Openings

1.b4 is a winning opening **http://www.sokolski.de/indexg.htm**
Chess Publishing **http://www.chesspublishing.com/**
Chessplayers' Inn **http://www.funet.fi/pub/doc/games/chess/**
Gambit Experts **http://www.thomasstock.com/gambit/expert.htm**
Infochess.com **http://www.infochess.com/**
La Regence Recent games arranged by opening
http://www.notzai.com/notzai/regence/regence.shtml
Thomas Johansson's website **http://hem.passagen.se/tjmisha/**
Winckelmann-Reimer Gambit home page **http://home.mira.net/~fludy/**

Chess Player Site

Alex Yermolinsky's webpage **http://www.concentric.net/~Yermo/**
Alexander Baburin's Chess Site **http://members.tripod.com/ababurin/**
Alexei Dreev: Chess View **http://dreev.da.ru**
An unofficial page on Viswanathan Anand
http://www.geocities.com/Colosseum/Slope/4448/
Bobby Fischer Homepage **http://www.rio.com/~johnnymc/**
Bobby Fischer Page **http://queen.chessclub.com/philchess/bobby.htm**
David Bronstein Navigator **http://davidbronstein.metropoli2000.net/**
Fan site about Peter Svidler **http://www.go.to/Svidler**
Grandmaster Gregory Kaidanov **http://members.iglou.com/kaidanov/**
Grandmaster Square **http://www.gmsquare.com/**
IM Attila Schneider's Chess Page **http://chessclinic.tripod.com/**
Jaan Ehlvest's homesite **http://www.ehlvest.com/**
Jon Levitt's Chess Pages **http://www.jlevitt.dircon.co.uk/**
Judit Polgar: Greatest Woman Chessplayer ever **http://www.controltheweb.com/polgar/**
Michael Adams (unofficial) Chess Site **http://www.geocities.com/thechesscorner/**
Mikhail Tal **http://www.jthin.co.uk/tal.htm**
Paul C. Dozsa **http://www.geocities.com/paldozsa/**
Rashid Ziatdinov's personal site **http://members.aol.com/Rziyatdino/HOME.html**
Ruslan Ponomariov **http://chess-sector.odessa.ua/ruslan.html**
Sergei Tiviakov's homepage. **http://www.tiviakov.demon.nl/index.htm**
Spraggett's Chess Wisdom **http://www.kevinspraggett.com**
Site about GM Peter Svidler **http://petersvidler.homestead.com/Pete.html**
The Chess of Peter Svidler **http://PeterSvidler.homestead.com/Pete.html**
The Chess of Rashid Nezhmetdinov **http://Nezhmetdinov.homestead.com/RGN.html**
The Chess of Vladimir Kramnik **http://kramnik.homestead.com/index.html**
Utut Adianto's site **http://www.ututadianto.com/**
Vishy Anand Chess Pages **http://www.geocities.com/Colosseum/Slope/4448/**

Chess Problems

BDS Site. Brian Stephenson's site on chess problems
http://www.bstephen.freeuk.com/index.html
BDS Web Site http://www.bstephen.freeuk.com/
Chess Problems Archive http://gpnm.iquebec.com/gpnm/
Chess Composition Books: Electronic editions of public domain works
http://www.algonet.se/~ath/
L'echecs http://www.synapse.net/~euler/echecs/index.htm
Nabokov's Chess Problems http://maskeret.com/italiascacchistica/a_nabokov.htm
Permanent Commission of the F.I.D.E. for Chess Compositions
http://www.saunalahti.fi/~stniekat/pccc/index.htm
Problemesis http://www.multimania.com/cpoisson/problemesis/
Problemiste (Shareware program for checking problems)
http://perso.easynet.fr/~mleschen/prb/problem.htm
Schachproblem Und Problemschach http://home.t-
online.de/home/ralf.kraetschmer/homepage.htm
Solving Chess by Lubomir Siran http://geocities.com/solvingchess/
Solving Chess Links http://geocities.com/solvingchess/links.html
Vaclav Kotesovec Problem links http://web.telecom.cz/vaclav.kotesovec/

Chess Publisher

Batsford Chess Books http://www.batsford.com/Chess
Chess Central http://www.chesscentral.com/
Chess City http://www.chesscity.com/
Everyman Books Page http://www.everyman.uk.com
Gambit Chess Publishers http://www.gambitchess.co.uk
McFarland & Company http://www.mcfarlandpub.com/
Schachverlag Kania http://www.kaniaverlag.de/
Smartchess Online http://www.smartchess.com/

Chess Ratings

Mauro Petrolo's ELO list search site http://www.mauro.sitehosting.net/cgi-
bin/elo/FIDE_search.asp

Chess Shop

Australian Chess Enterprises http://www.chessaustralia.com.au/
Beyer Verlag Online http://www.derschachladen.de/
Buch und Kunstantiquariat H. Schiffmann http://www.antiquariat-schiffmann.de/
Chess 4 Less http://www.chess4less.com/

Chess and Bridge Shop **http://www.chesscenter.com/shop/**
Chess Digest **http://www.chessdigest.com/**
Chessco chess shop **http://www.chessco.com/**
ChessEquipment.com **http://chessequipment.com/**
chessplayer.com **http://www.chessplayer.com/**
Chess-Shops.com **http://www.chess-shops.com/**
Chessware **http://www.chessware.de/**
Denksportboeken **http://www.denksportboeken.nl/**
Dusunsatranc Merkezi.com **http://www.dusunsatrancmerkezi.com/**
Eric Hallsworth Computer Chess Pages **http://www.elhchess.demon.co.uk/**
EURO SCHACH Dresden **http://www.euro-schach.de/**
Het Schaakbureau **http://www.code2.com/schaakbureau/**
Manchesster Supplies **http://www.manchesstersupplies.co.uk/**
Millennium 2000 **http://www.computerchess.com/**
Profischachladen Ralf-Axel Simon **http://www.schachsimon.de**
Schach Daniel **http://www.schach-daniel.com/**
Schach E. Niggemann **http://www.niggemann.com/**
Schach Markt **http://www.schachmarkt.de**
Schachantiquariat **http://www.schachwelt.de/Schachantiquariat**
SchachDepot Harald Wohlt **http://www.schachdepot.de/**
Schachladen im Altstadthof **http://www.schachladen-altstadthof.de/**
Schach-Profi-Verlag Reinhold Dreier **http://members.aol.com/DreierR/**
Schachversand Robert Ullrich **http://home.t-online.de/home/schachversand-ullrich**
Slav Chess Center **http://www.slavchess.co.il/**
Sticky Chess site **http://www.stickychess.com/**
Treasure Chess **http://members.aol.com/chess316/**
Your move chess and games **http://chessusa.com/**

Chess Software

Anjo Anjewierden **http://www.anjo.demon.nl/**
CBASCII Page **http://www.trojanco.demon.co.uk/cbascii/index.htm**
Cercle d'Échecs 'Fe Fou du Roi' **http://www.chez.com/lefouduroi/**
Chess Dragon **http://www.bluepaul.com/**
Chess Graphics **http://www.cowderoy.com/graphics/index.htm**
Chess Mentor **http://www.chess.com/**
Chess Program Reviews **http://www.chessreviews.com/**
Chess Software on Channel 1 **http://www.filelibrary.com/Contents/Multi-Platform/88/67.html**
Chess Software on TwoCows **http://easynet.games.tucows.com/chess.html**
Chess Source **http://www.chess-source.com/**
ChessMaker **http://www.alphaprime.com/chessmaker/**

EN PASSANT - Nørresundby Chess Club **http://www.enpassant.dk/chess/homeeng.htm**

Gambit Chess Site **http://www.gambitchess.com/**

Hasy's ChessWorld **http://www.hasy.de/**

Links to Mac Chess software

http://dmoz.org/Games/Board_Games/C/Chess/Software/Macintosh/

MacChess **http://members.aol.com/Macchess/**

Norresundby chess club **http://www.enpassant.dk/**

PGN Web Editor **http://lapides.tripod.com/pgnedit/pgnedit.html**

Rob Weir's ChessBase utilities for the old cbf format

http://www.cybercom.net/~rweir/cbutil16.htm

Sigma Chess Macintosh Chess Software. **http://www.sigmachess.com/**

SwissPerfect **http://www.swissperfect.com**

The University of Alberta GAMES Group **http://www.cs.ualberta.ca/~games/**

Traveller.com **http://misc.traveller.com/chess/**

True Type Chess Fonts **http://www.chessvariants.com/d.font/index.html**

U4Chess Page by Paul Onstad **http://www.sihope.com/~ponstad/**

University of Pittsburgh Archives **http://www.pitt.edu/~schach/Archives/index2.html**

Chess Software: Database

Bookup **http://www.bookup.com**

CDB **http://www.chessopolis.com/csr/cdb_10.htm**

Chess Assistant **http://www.chessassistant.com**

ChessBase **http://www.chessbase.com**

ChessBase German Page **http://www.chessbase.de/**

ChessBase Spanish Page **http://www.chessbase.com/elturco/index.htm**

Scid 'Shane's Chess Information Database' **http://members.xoom.com/sghudson/**

TASC **http://www.tasc.nl**

Chess Software: Electronic

Electronic Chess Books **http://www.echessbook.com/**

Chess Software: License

GNU General Public License **http://www.fsf.org/copyleft/gpl.html**

Chess Software: PGN Reader

ChessBase Lite **http://www.chessbase.com/Products/cblight/index.htm**

PGN Read by Keith Fuller **http://members.aol.com/keithfx/**

Talanto Chess Viewer **http://www.chessviewer.com**

Microsoft's PGN Viewer

http://www.microsoft.com/DirectX/dxm/samples/Multimedia/danim/java/apps/chess/Chess.html

Chess Software: Mac

Sigma Chess Macintosh Chess Software **http://www.sigmachess.com/**

Chess Variants

The Chess Variant Pages **http://www.chessvariants.com/**

Commercial Site

Sticky Chess **http://www.stickychess.com/**

Computer Chess

A tribute to Winboard **http://www.inficad.com/~ecollins/winboard.htm**
Andy's Roundabout **http://www.andreas-schwartmann.de/**
Arasan chess by Jon Dart **http://www.best.com/~jdart/arasan.htm**
Archives of the Kasparov vs Deep Blue Rematch **http://www.research.ibm.com/deepblue/**
Chenard by Don Cross **http://www.intersrv.com/~dcross/chenard.html**
Chess Freeware and Shareware Download Page
http://webhome.globalserve.net/chess/chesprgs.htm
Chess Programming Links **http://www.xs4all.nl/~verhelst/chess/programming.html**
Chessbase Winboard Adapter
http://www.chessbase.com/Products/engines/winboard/adapter.htm
ChessFiz and Holmes by Andreas Herrmann **http://www.wbholmes.de/**
Chessfuns Computer Chess Webpages **http://www.geocities.com/chessfun_1999/**
ChessMaster **http://www.chessmaster.com/**
Chessopolis: Computer Chess **http://www.chessopolis.com/cchess.htm**
Computer Chess RATINGS from Selective Search Magazine
http://www.elhchess.demon.co.uk/ehss.htm
Computer Schach Site **http://www.computerschach.de/**
Crafty Benchmark Page **http://homes.dsl.nl/~rudolf/craftybench.html**
Crafty Download Page **ftp://ftp.cis.uab.edu/pub/hyatt**
Five piece endings **http://wwwjn.inf.ethz.ch/games/chess/**
Frank's Chess Page **http://amateurschach.in-trier.de/**
Gambit-Soft Homepage **http://www.gambitsoft.com/**
GromitChess Home Page **http://home.t-online.de/home/hobblefrank/**
Hossa - A Chess Program by Steffen A. Jakob **http://www.jakob.at/steffen/hossa.html**
How to use Crafty with Winboard **http://cafelatte.freeservers.com/chess/**
IBM Deep Blue site **http://www.research.ibm.com/deepblue/**
International Computer Chess Association **http://www.dcs.qmw.ac.uk/~icca/**

Kchess **http://www.arkangles.com/kchess.htm**
Ken Thompson **http://cm.bell-labs.com/who/ken/index.html**
Komputer Korner **http://www.gambitsoft.com/komputer.htm**
Konfiguration von WinBoard-Engines **http://www.ginko.de/user/volker.pittlik/schach/a-config.htm**
maro's Rebel Support Page
http://www.geocities.com/CapeCanaveral/Launchpad/2640/rebel.htm
Nero by Jari Huikari **http://www.mit.jyu.fi/~huikari/download.html**
PermanentBrain's Site **http://meineseite.i-one.at/PermanentBrain/**
Rebel Software Site **http://www.rebel.nl/**
Rival Chess **http://dialspace.dial.pipex.com/chris.moreton/software.shtml**
The Swedish Chess Computer Association **http://home.swipnet.se/~w-36794/ssdf/**
Tim Mann author of Winboard/Xboard.
http://www.research.digital.com/SRC/personal/Tim_Mann/chess.html
Tony's Chess Site **http://home.interact.se/~w100107/welcome.htm**
Winboard/Xboard Pages **http://www.research.digital.com/SRC/personal/mann/xboard.html**
Winchess **http://rocketdownload.com/details/stra/winchess.htm**

Correspondence Chess

All Service Postal Chess Club **http://bluemoon.net/~georgbar/noframes.htm**
American Postal Chess Tournaments (APCT) **http://correspondencechess.com/apct/**
British Correspondence Chess Association **http://www.dbsugden.clara.net/**
Chess Journalists of American **http://www.correspondencechess.com/cja/aw2000.htm**
Chess Mail **http://www.chessmail.com/**
Chess Pages of Mike Donnelly. **http://ourworld-top.cs.com/DrMJDonnelly/index.htm**
Correspondence Chess League of America Web Site **http://www.emailchess.net/**
Correspondencechess.com **http://correspondencechess.com/**
Der deutsche E-Mail-Schachclub **http://desc.purespace.de/desc.htm**
Deutscher Fernschachbund (BdF) **http://www.fernschach.de**
Egbert Bösenberg Homepage **http://home.t-online.de/home/EBoesenberg/britain.htm**
e-mail Chess Federation **http://www.geocities.com/email_chess/**
Fernschach International (Magazin) **http://www.fschach.mtl.pl/**
International Correspondence Chess Federation. US site. **http://www.iccfus.com/**
International Email Chess Club **http://www.geocities.com/Colosseum/Midfield/1264/**
International Email Chess Group **http://www.iecg.org/**
Italian Correspondence Chess Association **http://www.asigc.it/**
MyEmailChess.com **http://www.myemailchess.com/**
Playchess.de **http://www.playchess.de/playchess.htm**
Portuguese Correspondence Chess Federation **http://planeta.clix.pt/cnxc**
Ralph Marconi's Chess Site **http://correspondencechess.com/marconi/**
Raymond Boger Chess Web **http://home.c2i.net/w-328768/my_chess_web/startsiden.htm**

Stephan Busemann Correspondence Chess Grandmaster
http://cl-www.dfki.uni-sb.de/~busemann/schach.html
The British Correspondence Chess Society
http://communities.msn.co.uk/TheBritishCorrespondenceChessSociety/
The Campbell Report Correspondence Chess **http://correspondencechess.com/campbell/**
The Chess Web Page of Frederic Fricot **http://www.chez.com/emailchess/**
The International Correspondence Chess Federation **http://www.iccf.com/**
Thinks Guide to Correspondence Chess **http://thinks.com/webguide/chess-corr.htm**
UNIVERSAL EMAIL CHESS CLUB **http://www.lobocom.es/~ebailen/cmain.html**
US Chess On-line. Correspondence Chess **http://www.uschess.org/cc/index.html**
World Correspondence Chess Federation **http://www.geocities.com/radale/wccf/**

Discussion Board

Gamers.com chess board
http://boards.gamers.com/messages/overview.asp?name=RealWT&page=1

FIDE Ratings

Searchable FIDE rating list **http://www.rhrk.uni-kl.de/~wehner/fide.html**

General Chess Interest

'Mieux jouer aux Echecs' **http://www.mjae.com/reyes/index.html**
Aalborg Skakforening. Fun, fun, fun. **http://www.business.auc.dk/~gv/chess/fun.html**
Bill Wall's Chess Page **http://www.geocities.com/SiliconValley/Lab/7378/chess.htm**
Braingames.net **http://www.braingames.net/**
Chaturanga (Brilliancy Prizes in Chess) **http://www.multimania.com/chaturanga/**
Chess Addicts **http://www.chessaddict.com**
Chess Archaeology **http://www.chessarch.com/arch.shtml**
Chess Banner Network **http://banners.fide.com/**
Chess Café Site **http://www.chesscafe.com/**
Chess History Center **http://www.chesshistory.com/**
Chess Journalists of America **http://correspondencechess.com/cja/**
ChessMoves **http://www.bcf.ndirect.co.uk/chessmoves/**
Chess related comic-strips **http://www.inficad.com/~ecollins/chess-comics.htm**
Chesscorner.com **http://www.chesscorner.com/**
CHESSDON **http://www.chessdon.com/**
Chessnia **http://www.chessnia.com/**
ChessWorks Homepage (Eric Schiller's Homepage **http://www.chessworks.com/**
David Cohen's Chess trivia site **http://www.ncf.carleton.ca/~bw998/index.html**
Ed's ever growing chess page. **http://www.edcollins.com/chess/**
G. Ossimitz: Chess Page **http://www.crosswinds.net/~ossimitz/chess.htm**

Chess on the Net

Glensdad Homepage **http://www.mindspring.com/~imbusy/chess/_chess.htm**
Goddess Chess Pages **http://www.goddesschess.com/**
Grandmaster Corner **http://www.grandmastercorner.com**
Ignacio Marin's Chess Page **http://cmgm.stanford.edu/~marin/chess.html**
inChess.com World News **http://www.inchess.com/**
Kaissiber **http://www.kaissiber.de/**
Kasparov vs The World Site **http://www.zone.com/kasparov/**
Kasparov.com in Russia **http://www.kasparovchess.ru/**
Kasparovchess.com **http://www.kasparovchess.com/**
Klub Karpov **http://www.geocities.com/WallStreet/District/9917/klubkarpov.html**
KramnikOnline **http://www.kramnikonline.com**
Live Chess on the Internet Sites **http://chess.liveonthenet.com/**
Mats Winther's chess site **http://hem.passagen.se/melki9/**
Max Euwe-Centrum in Amsterdam **http://www.maxeuwe.nl/**
MECCA Chess Encyclopedia **http://maskeret.com/mecca/index.shtml**
Mind Sports Olympiad Chess pages **http://www.msoworld.com/mindzine/news/Chess**
Mind Sports Olympiad site **http://www.msoworld.com/**
Mr Chess **http://www.redweb.com/chess/**
National Chess Network Life Master Brian McCarthy and associates.
http://hometown.aol.com/bmcc333/bmcc.html
Palamede **http://www.palamede.com/**
Randy's Revealing Reviews **http://ourworld.compuserve.com/homepages/randybauer/**
Sam Sloan's Chess Page **http://www.ishipress.com/chess.htm**
Sam Sloan's Chess Page **http://www.samsloan.com/chess.htm**
Schach! **http://www.schachmatt.de**
Schachecke **http://www.schachecke.de**
Schachreisen Jörg Hickl **http://www.joerg-hickl.de/**
Schachwelt **http://www.schachwelt.de**
Scott McCloud Chess Cartoon **http://www.scottmccloud.com/comics/chess/chess.html**
Tacky Patzer Chess **http://zip.to/jeroen**
Tales Of 1001 Knights **http://www.1001knights.com/**
The Chicken Factor **http://chesswise.com/Chickenfactor.htm**
Tiger Chess **http://www.tigerchess.com/**
Tim Krabbé's Chess Curiosities **http://www.xs4all.nl/~timkr/chess/chess.html**
TNQ Sponsorship exclusively represents the commercial interests of Viswanathan Anand
in India **http://www.tnqsponsorship.com/vishwa.html**
Tor's academic survey into how chess players think **http://www.delight.dk/chess/**
Uncrowned Kings **http://www.phileo.demon.co.uk/**
US Chess Hall of Fame **http://www.chesslinks.org/hof/**

Internet Chat

IRCUsers.com **http://www.newircusers.com/**

Internet Chess Guide

about.com on chess **http://chess.about.com/**
Quebecois Chess **http://fqechecs.qc.ca/sites/sitesquebecois.htm**

Java Viewer

Chess Tutor site. **http://members.nbci.com/esuastegui/eschess/**
Misty Beach PGN Viewer Applet **http://www.mistybeach.com/products/PGNViewer/**
MyChess site **http://www.mychess.com**

Javascript Viewer

Palview **http://www.cowderoy.com/chess/palview/**

Mailing lists

About.chess mailing list
http://chess.about.com/games/chess/gi/pages/mmail.htm?page=subscribe
Chess Express Mailing list mailto:IWANTCHESSEXPRESS@keepAhead.com
Chess Mailing List **http://tom.cuy.net/chess/**

Newspaper Chess Column

El Pais **http://www.elpais.es/**
La Nación y para una radio Continental. Ajedrez section **http://www.tyc.com.ar/**
Liberation Newspaper **http://www.liberation.fr/echecs/index.html**
Lubosh Kavalek's Washington Post Column **http://www.washingtonpost.com/wp-dyn/style/columns/chess/**
Max Pam's chess columns for Parool **http://www.maxpam.nl/index1.html**
New York Times **http://www.nytimes.com/diversions/chess/**
Red Star Newspaper Chess Column **http://www.redstar.ru/chess.html**
Sentinel and Enterprise Newspaper **http://www.sentinelandenterprise.com**
The Hindu Newspaper **http://www.the-hindu.com/**
Algemeen Dagblad column by Tim Krabbe **http://people.a2000.nl/tkrabbe/admag**
The Times **http://www.thetimes.co.uk/**
Transylvania Times Chess Column by Malcolm Young
http://www.malcolmyoung.com/Chess%20Pages/chess.htm

On-line Chess

Caissa's Web **http://caissa.com/**
chess.net **http://chess.net/**
chess.net Java client **http://www.chess.net/play/java**
ChessWeb **http://studwww.rug.ac.be/~mjdbruyn/chessweb/**
Dr Unclear's Homepage
http://www.geocities.com/Area51/Realm/8655/ENGLISH/Main_ENG.htm
Dutch ICS **http://www.dds.nl/~schaak/**
Free ICS **http://www.freechess.org/**
German Internet Server **http://www.unix-ag.uni-kl.de/~chess/**
Internet Chess Club **http://www.chessclub.com/**
Links to Free ICS servers **http://www.freechess.org/link.html**
On-line games site **http://www.2am.com/**
The Slow Time Control Bunch. **http://www.continet.com/ckmate/STC-Bunch/STCHome.html**
World Blitz Chess Association **http://hometown.aol.com/wbcablitz/main.html**
Yahoo Games includes chess **http://games.yahoo.com/top/index.html**
Yahoo! Chess vs. The Chess Servers **http://www.inficad.com/~ecollins/yahoo-vs-servers.htm**
Zook's Pagina **http://www.zook.tmfweb.nl/**

On-line Chess: Java

Achess.com **http://www.achess.com/**
Chessed Site **http://www.chessed.com/**
ItsYourTurn.com **http://itsyourturn.com/**
Microsoft gaming zone **http://www.zone.com**
Pogo.com **http://www.pogo.com/**
Vinco Online Games **http://www.vog.ru/**
World Chess Network **http://www.worldchessnetwork.com/**

On-line translations

Babel Fish Page **http://world.altavista.com**
Free Translation.com **http://www.freetranslation.com/**
Systran Powered on-line translator **http://translator.go.com/**

PGN Standard

PGN Standard **http://www.schachprobleme.de/chessml/faq/pgn/**
PGN Standard **http://www.very-best.de/pgn-spec.htm**
PGN Standard **http://www.chessclub.com/help/PGN-spec**

Regional Chess

Canadian Chess **http://www.ncf.carleton.ca/~bw998/canchess.html**

chesstalk.com **http://www.chesstalk.com/**

Federacion Ajedrez Vincente Lopez **http://escavm.tripod.com/**

Hampshire Chess Association **http://www.hampshirechess.co.uk/**

Illinois (USA) Chess Association **http://www.illinoischess.org/icahome/**

Karpov Chess Centre in Baden Baden **http://www.karpow-schachzentrum.de/**

Massachusetts Chess Association **http://www.masschess.org**

Nebraska Chess History **http://www.huntel.net/jjirous/jjirous.htm**

North Circular Chess League **http://www.users.globalnet.co.uk/~cernunos/nccl.htm**

Chess in El Salvador **http://esajedrez.tripod.com**

Southern Counties Chess Union **http://www.sccu.ndo.co.uk/**

The Manchester Chess Scene **http://www.adamsfam.demon.co.uk/**

Tucson Chess Magazine **http://www.azstarnet.com/~m8n2/index.html**

Ulster Chess Chronicle **http://www.rct26.dial.pipex.com/**

Yorkshire Chess Unofficial page by Steve Mann **http://members.madasafish.com/~sjmann/**

Glossary

Alta Vista A popular search engine.

anonymous ftp See ftp

archive A single file that contains a group of files which have been compressed for easier storage and speedier downloading.

arg file A type of compressed file.

attachment A computer file which is fastened to and sent with an email.

binary file A computer file containing information which doesn't consist of just plain text. Instead it may, for example, contain a picture, sounds, or a word processing document with formatting.

browser A computer program with a graphical user interface which allows you to view web pages on the World Wide Web.

chat There are a number of programs and networks on the Internet where you can communicate in real time with other people on-line. Examples are ICQ (I seek you) and IRC (Internet relay chat).

chess engine The part of a chess playing computer that calculates the moves. Sometimes chess playing programs will allow different engines to be used with the same product or program.

chess server A computer which is set up so that you can log on and play chess.

chess client A program that makes it easier for you to play chess on the Internet. It's perfectly possible to play chess by connecting to a chess server by telnet and then issue commands line by line. A client usually a graphical user interface makes it much easier and·pleasant to play chess by hiding these commands and displaying the moves on a graphics board.

compression Files can be made much smaller or compressed so they can be more quickly transmitted over the Internet. There are different programs that carry this process out. The most commonly used on the Internet is the zip format. You need a program capable of restoring the files once you have downloaded them. ChessBase has its own compression program that produces a .cbv file which can be also unpacked by Chess-Base.

demo version Demo or demonstration versions of software are made available so you can try the software and see if you like it. Not all the features of the program will work.

DNS Domain Name System Addresses on the Internet are really in the form of numbers called IP addresses. It is preferable to have these addresses in the form of names. Every time you use a name e.g. **http://www.microsoft.com** the DNS translates it into the IP address 207.46.230.218 so that the website can be found.

download To copy files from a remote computer to your own.

freeware Software which is available for use free of charge. There may be limitations if you intend to use the program commercially however.

FTP (file transfer protocol) This is the standard used on the Internet for sending files. All computers you connect to require a user name and password. Some are set up to allow anyone to connect. These are called anonymous ftp servers. You log in with a username of anonymous and a password, which is your email address.

GIF An electronic format for images.

GNU A project to supply free public software (**http://www.gnu.org**).

GUI Graphical User Interface. This is a program that makes it easier to use computers. Instead of issuing text commands you can click buttons and icons.

handle A nickname chosen by a user (see Playing on the Net, Chapter 3).

HTML Hypertext Mark-up Language. A standard used for creating and displaying web pages.

HTTP Hypertext Transfer Protocol. A standard used for the transmission and receipt of documents and files on the Internet, defining what action the computers involved should take.

hypertext A form of text which allows navigation links between a picture or text to other documents or different parts of the same document.

Interface A program that stands between you and a computer and issues and interprets commands in a way you can understand.

Internet The connection of Computers worldwide, allowing them to communicate with each other.

Internet Explorer A very popular web browser which is found in Microsoft Windows.

InterNIC An organisation with a number of purposes the most high profile being the registration of domain names.

Chess on the Net

IRC Internet Relay Chat.

IP Address An identifying address for a computer on the Internet.

ISP An Internet Service Provider is a company or organisation which provides access to the Internet.

Java A programming language similar to C. It can be used both for regular programming tasks but it has been adopted as the standard programming language for programs that will run from inside a browser.

Javascript A scripting language which allows Web authors to design interactive sites.

JPEG An electronic format for images.

mailing list A list of email addresses which can be identified by a single name. When an email message is sent to the mailing list it is automatically forwarded to all the addresses in the list.

modem Short for modulator-demodulator. A modem is a device that enables a computer to transmit data over telephone lines.

Netscape Navigator Another popular web browser.

news server A news server provides access to newsgroups. Most ISP's have their own news server but some don't, in which case you'll have to find one you can subscribe to.

newsgroup An open forum on the Internet, which is a kind of open email that can be read by anyone who subscribes to the topic you are posting in.

newsreader The raw messages in newsgroups are not very easy to follow. A newsreader arranges the messages so that those on the same topic appear together in a thread.

PC Personal Computer

PDF file A file format for documents which can be read by Adobe Acrobat. You can download a reader for free from Adobe's site **http://www.adobe.com/acrobat**.

PGN Short for Portable Game Notation, the standard format for transmitting games around the Internet.

protocol An agreed-upon format for transmitting data between two computers.

server A computer that stores files and runs programs, allowing them to be accessed on the Internet in some way.

search engine A program that allows you to search either a site or internet index for words that interest you, giving you the result in the form of references to sites where those terms occur.

shareware Software distributed on the basis that if you make use of it regularly you would pay a fee (usually a small one) for it, although it is up to the user to decide whether they honour this implicit agreement. Sometimes extra features or annoying reminders you haven't paid for the software are removed on payment.

Telnet A Telnet program runs on your computer and allows you to connect to remote computers and issue commands. It works in real time so it allows direct communication with other people logged on to that same remote computer.

Thread A thread is a series of newsgroup posting all on the same topic. Someone will start the topic and the rest of the thread will consist of those messages that reply to the original posting or the responses.

upload The opposite of downloading. This is the process of transferring a file from a personal computer to a computer on the Internet, so that others can have access to it.

URL Uniform Resource Locator. A web address.

Usenet Another name for newsgroups.

virus A program (usually very small) which replicates itself and if allowed passes itself on to other computers, either by floppy disk or the Internet. Not all viruses cause serious damage to computer systems but many do. You should buy an anti-virus program and keep it up to date if you use the Internet.

web site A location on the World Wide Web. Every site has a home page (by default, but not infallibly index.html or index.htm) which may connect to other single web pages.

web page A single page on a web site.

Winzip The most popular program for zipping and unzipping compressed files. It can also deal with other compression formats.

Webopedia You can look up computing terms you are unsure about in an on-line computer and technology dictionary at: **http://www.webopedia.com**.

World Wide Web A concept harder to define than understand. It stems from the development of the Internet browser. Could be defined as a global network based hypertext information system that uses the Internet to transmit, amongst other things, graphical, video, textual, and audio information.

ZIP file A type of compressed file.